Arthur Asa Berger

Culture Codes

Butt Fiends, Big Macs, Playboys, Jokes, the Super Bowl, Popular Music, Love, and other curiosities of American culture and society.

Marin Arts Press
Mill Valley, California

Copyright © Arthur Asa Berger   2012
All Rights Reserved
ISBN-10: 1481900090
ISBN-13: 9781480090194
Library of Congress number: 10 293190

Contents

It was then that I began to learn how any problem, whether grave or trivial, can be resolved.   The method never varies.   First, you establish the traditional "two views" of the question.   You then put forward a commonsense justification of the one, only to refute it by the other. Finally you send them both packing by use of a third interpretation in which both the others are shown to be equally unsatisfactory. Certain verbal manoeuvres enable you, that is, to line up the traditional "antitheses" as complementary aspects of a single reality: form and substance, content and container, appearance and reality, essence and existence, continuity and discontinuity, and so on.   Before long the exercise becomes the merest verbalizing, reflection gives place to a kind of superior punning, and the "accomplished philosopher" maybe be recognized by the ingenuity with which he makes ever bolder play with assonance, ambiguity, and the use of those words which sound alike and yet bear quite different meanings.

Claude Lévi-Strauss.   *Tristes Tropiques.*   Translated by John Russell. New York: Athaneum. 1955/1970. page 70.

Introduction

I don't recall when I got the idea for writing a book on *culture codes* but I know that on Saturday, August 1, 1998 I devoted a page in my journal, Volume 70, to the topic. I made a chart in which I listed various attributes of codes such as: levels, manifestations, specific examples, problems with the concept, and topics that I might want to discuss. Usually, when I devote a page to a topic it is because I have been thinking about it, off and on, for a while.

The brainstorming I did on codes evolved and led to some speculations about the nature of codes and how they might be found in various aspects of life. Over the years I worked on the topic, off and on, and a few years after I did the page on codes I wrote a book which I called *Culture Codes*. My thesis was that much of our behavior is structured and follows certain codes, most of which function below our level of awareness.

My speculations were on a very high level of abstraction and I listed topics to be investigated and written about. In my book I didn't develop every topic on this page. For example, I didn't develop my ideas about the levels of codes as much as I might have. In this page from my journals I speculated about the levels at which codes operate. Some codes are universal—such as the seven facial expressions (and one that is neutral) that psychologist Paul Ekman discovered when he did research into the matter. He discovered that while there are a large number of facial expressions, only seven facial expressions are universal and are found everywhere. Some codes are area-wide, and can be found in Western Europe or Southeast Asia, for example.

In Southeast Asia, the code for "starch to be eaten with

meals" is rice.   Some codes are national and are located primarily in nation states such as the United States, France, China or any other country. At a level below the national we find regional codes. In the United States, for example, regions such as New England, the Pacific Northwest, and the Deep South, have different codes for foods, the people there have different accents and the codes that are dominant differ in many ways from national codes found in the United States.

One can move further down the scale and find cities that have distinct codes such as San Francisco and then parts of San Francisco such as the Mission or Pacific Heights, where there are area-specific sub codes. Finally, we can deal with individuals, whose ideas and behaviors are shaped by the codes they have absorbed, often at the unconscious level (described by Clotaire Rapaille, a cultural anthropologist and marketing consultant as "imprinting").

Another list on the page deals with "Rituals" that can be seen as codes. These rituals involve meals we eat, dating, gift giving, shopping and many other structured activities that are part of our daily lives. I also speculate about kinds of codes: some are formal while others are informal; some are covert and hidden while others are manifest; some are constant and others are occasional. You can see, then, that there are many different aspects of what I call *culture codes* to deal with.   After reading this book I think you will have an appreciation of the role that *culture codes* play in our lives, our societies and our cultures.   My speculations in 1998 led, eventually, to this book. I wrote a number of books between 1998 and the present, but I always had this notion that I might expand my chart into a book. This shows that the creative process is a complex and curious matter and that sometimes ideas germinate in one's head for years or even decades before they end up in books.

All of the different codes for all of the different imprints, when put together, create a reference system that people living in these cultures use without being aware of it.   These reference systems guide different cultures in very different ways. If you have all the right numbers in the right sequence, you can open the lock. Doing so over a vast array of imprints has profound implications. It brings to us the answer to one of our most fundamental questions: why do we act the way we do?   Understanding the Culture Code provides us with a remarkable new tool—a new set of glasses, if you will, with which to view ourselves and our behaviors. It changes the way we see everything around us. What's more, it confirms what we have always suspected is t rue—that, despite our common humanity, people around the world really *are* different.   The Culture Code offers a way to understand how.... Most of us imprint the meanings of the things most central to our lives by the age of seven. This is because emotion is the central force for children under the age of seven...An imprint and its Code are like a lock and its combination

Clotaire Rapaille. *The Culture Code.* New York: Broadway Books. 2006:10-11, 22.

Chapter 1:

Culture Codes

In this book I suggest that cultures can be thought of as collections of codes that shape our behavior. Codes that we are aware of we call "rules" or "laws," but codes that we do not recognize, but which shape our thinking and behavior in many areas, I call *culture codes*. I explain the various characteristics of these codes below. We know that genetic codes play a major role in shaping our physical bodies and in many illnesses we are plagued with. In the same light, *culture codes* play a major role in our thoughts and behavior, even though we generally are not aware of the existence of these codes. I made a caricature of myself as a "code breaker" and "code finder" and "code analyst" in which I took on the persona of "Decoder Man."

Characteristics of Codes

Codes are in fashion for the moment (code a la mode). You see mention of codes in most of the avant garde writings of semioticians, ethnomethodologists, linguists, psychologists, anthropologists, and various other kinds of social scientists and humanities scholars. The notion is that many aspects of our lives have a hidden or internal "logic" and structure and are shaped in some ways we do not generally recognize. Generally speaking, they are in our unconscious. As Freud explained in his article "Psychoanalysis" (1963):

> It was a triumph for the interpretative art of psychoanalysis when it succeeded in demonstrating that certain common mental acts of normal people, for which no one had hitherto attempted to put forward a psychological explanation, were to be regarded in the same light as the symptoms of neurotics: that is to say they had a *meaning,* which was unknown to the subject but which could easily be discovered by analytic means. .
> . . A class of material was brought to light which is calculated better than any other to stimulate a belief in the existence of unconscious mental acts even in people to whom the hypothesis of something at once mental and unconscious seems strange and even absurd. (pp.-235–236)

So something can be in our minds but we are not conscious that this is so. Later in the book I offer a quotation from a marketing professor at Harvard, Gerald Zaltman, to the effect that we are conscious of only five percent of what is in our minds and our behavior is profoundly affected by the ninety-five percent, in our unconscious.

> But what is a code? In spy literature much use is made of scrambled messages which can only be unlocked by knowing a certain code—that is, by knowing what stands for what. Consider the following letters that don't seem to mean anything:

D V M U V S F   D P E F T

The code for unlocking the meaning of these letters is *minus* 1. When we apply this code to these letters we get

D V M U V S F   D P E F T

Minus 1

C U L T U R E   C O D E S

So things that might seem trivial or meaningless often appear that way to us because we do not know the codes that unlock their meaning.

The *Concise Oxford Dictionary* defines a code as a "set of letters or figures or word groups with arbitrary meanings for brevity or secrecy." If you look at transcripts of messages sent by texters you find many abbreviations and strange constructions that are now conventionally used. Another definition of a code is a "systematic collection of statutes, body of laws so arranged as to avoid inconsistency and overlapping." If we combine the two meanings and apply them to culture we have a pretty good way of understanding *culture codes*. Codes are, in essence, instructions sent to us by our cultures, which, in some cases, are disguised so we do not understand their significance. But I would like to say a bit more about them. The code for the material that follows is "begin with a C."

Codes are coherent.
Implicit in the very definition of a code is the notion of coherence, the notion that for a code to be a code the things it codifies have to be related in some systematic way. We are very close here to the so-called "coherence theory of truth," except that the relations are arbitrary for a given sphere and nothing is necessarily related to anything else, except within the sphere covered by the code. Relations are necessary only because the code defines them that way. The coherence theory of truth of the Absolute Idealists stated that there were degrees of truth, and some truths were more true than others in that they explained more about reality than weak truths did. If everything is related to everything else then knowing anything

enables you, ultimately, to know everything. You can work it out for yourself—if, that is, you know *how* everything is related to everything else.   In Conan Doyle's "*A Study in Scarlet*" there is a passage that is relevant:

> Its somewhat ambitious title was *The Book of Life,* and it attempted to show how much an observant man might learn by an accurate and systematic examination of all that came in his way. It struck me as being a remarkable mixture of shrewdness and of absurdity. The reasoning was close and intense, but the deductions appeared to me to be far-fetched and exaggerated .

> "From a drop of water," said the writer, "a logician could infer the possibility of an Atlantic or a Niagara without having seen or heard of one or the other. *So all life is a great chain, the nature of which is known whenever we are shown a single link of it.*" [My Italics]

From a drop of water we can infer the existence of our rivers and oceans and all kinds of other things.

Cultures can be seen as collections of codes.
Every culture can be thought of, as a collection of codes of conduct and these codes are transmitted from one generation to another. I am using culture here anthropologically—not as some people do when they are dealing with aesthetic considerations. Everyone has a culture, then—
though everyone doesn't necessarily appreciate *elite* culture—ballet, chamber music, poetry, avant-garde literature, and other art forms that require sophisticated and educated aesthetic sensibilities. I will consider the terms *culture, codes* and *culture-codes* to be synonymous for our purposes henceforth. Cultures provide us with "ways of behaving" in various situations and ways of looking at the world and society and man, and these ways all these considerations lock together to form a coherent system for each culture (or sub-culture). We know from the work of Basil Bernstein that children pickup, almost by osmosis it seems, attitudes toward time and themselves and the world bymeans of the codes hidden in the language of their parents and peers.
        This leads to the next consideration—codes are covert.

Codes are covert.

People are generally not aware of the extent to which their actions (and thoughts) and behaviors are "governed" or "shaped" by their culture. All of this is unconscious and unrecognized by them. We are, as Rapaille puts it, "imprinted" when we are children with certain codes. A culture is a code and is, therefore. to a great degree, "secret"— at least to the people involved who have been "enculturated." When people become aware of cultural codes they can modify them and arrange them to suit their purposes. In such cases culture as a code loses its power to shape behavior the way it did before the code was discovered.

Pierre Bourdieu uses the notion "cultural unconscious" and explains its relation to individuals as follows:

> It may seem surprising to ascribe to the cultural unconscious the attitudes, aptitudes, knowledge, themes and problems, in short the whole system of categories of perception and thought acquired by the systematic apprenticeship which the school organizes or makes it possible to organize. This is because the creator maintains with his acquired culture, as with his early culture, a relationship which might be defined according to Nicolai Hartmann as both "carrying" and "being carried" and he is not aware that the culture he possesses possesses him. ["Intellectual Field and Creative Project."]

The relationship between individual and cultures is a complex one, for we both shape our cultures and are shaped by it. The important point for us to consider, however, is that individuals are frequently "unaware" of the extent to which our culture "possesses us." To paraphrase Emile Durkheim, we are in society and society is in us.

Codes are concrete.

For a culture to maintain itself (and I will say something about the problem of change later), it must relate to concrete and specific matters. What do you do when a baby cries? Every culture has an answer for this which is related to the specific situation in which the crying occurs. In one cultural tradition you give the baby a teaspoon of olive oil. When I lived in Italy, the woman who owned our apartment explained to me that bodies are machines and need oil to run well; in another you feed the baby; in another (if it is not four hours since he was last fed) you let babies cry, until they pass out from exhaustion, having been traumatized and experienced starvation at a very early age. The imprint of this starvation lives with them the rest of their lives.

For a code to work it must be specific; and the power of *culture codes* is directly related to their capacity to help or guide people in different situations, and to give detailed and rigorous rules for any given situation. If a code is not concrete people will start improvising; and when they do, the culture, as a coherent system, is in danger of falling apart. This, in turn, suggests the next attribute of cultural codes—they must be clear.

Codes must be clear

Not only must codes deal with specific matters in specific ways; people must be, to the extent it is possible, clear about what they are to do. This need for clarity is connected with the matter of concreteness. People must know how they are to deal with particular situations they face at various times. A cookbook would be a good example of the need for concreteness and clarity. It is most specific about the contents of a given recipe and about how the contents are to be combined and cooked. It is also generates a kind of code, in that certain dishes are combined with others and these combinations, though arbitrary and culturally specific (or sub-culturally specific) are seen as correct, and natural. They are in the real of that which goes without question.

The English eat great quantities of fish and Brussels sprouts, but when in England one does not see restaurants featuring "Fish and Sprouts" or "Fish and Carrots" or even "Fish and Baked Potatoes." A national cuisine is a code, also. (Barthes sees it as a "signifying system" with rules of association, exclusion, etc.). People absorb (literally as well as figuratively) this code and seldom question it. Some people, as the result of travel or marriage to people from different cultures, move beyond their cultural food codes, but most do not. Anthropologists report that food preferences are created in our earliest years and tend to shape what we eat for the rest of our lives.

Thus, this unacknowledged code system that we know of as culture must be invisible to us and yet, at the same time, give clear and unambiguous answers about hot to deal with specific problems. This tension within a culture is further complicated by the matter of change and continuity in cultures.

Codes must have continuity.

It is only logical that cultures must have continuity and lasting power, otherwise the very idea of culture and *cultural codes* is compromised. On the other hand, cultures are subjected to pressures (brought on by social changes, historical accidents, etc.) so they must be able to change, also—but they cannot change too fast lest they lose their identity or coherence. When we use the word "tradition" we are really talking about the continuity of a culture, its capacity to shape people's expectations and ideas about what is correct and valuable.

Cultures face the dilemma, then, of mediating between the internal need for continuity and maintenance and the external pressure to change and accommodate to new situations, which may be a condition for survival. Sometimes this matter is solved through the creation of sub-cultures, which siphon off discontented elements into little entities at variance in certain respects to the main culture but which do not, necessarily, aim at overthrowing it. Other times, however, counter-cultures arise which are antagonistic to the central culture and which engage it in a fight for survival—a fight which sometimes is successful, but which frequently leads to relatively minor modifications in the main culture that enable it to weather the storm.

Codes must have continuity but they must also face the need of being changed and probably can be best characterized as being in a state of dynamic equilibrium.

Codes are Comprehensive.

Culture strives towards totality; it must cover as much of a given person's world of experience (or a society's) as it can. It is this comprehensiveness which helps account for its invisibility. Because cultural codes are everywhere we take no notice of them; it is a case of fish not being aware of water. It is their total environment and so becomes invisible. They cannot get away from it and take it into account. In the realm of politics, this invisibility is described as hegemonial ideological domination by Gramsci and Marxists.

This comprehensiveness is implicit in the definition of a code. A code which did not tell how to understand every figure or word group in a coded message would not be very useful, though a good cryptologist could no doubt deduce or derive the whole code from knowing part of it. *Cultural codes* are a different matter, however. Within their sphere (nations, regions, classes, etc.) codes must be comprehensive to function without being noticed.

Let us return to our example of food systems or codes. Not only do we pick up from the code ideas about what foods are good to eat and what foods go with other foods, we also gain notions about the order in which foods should be served, how a "complete" meal should be started and ended. In the United States, for example, we don't serve boiled potatoes with steak, and we broil or grill steaks rather than boil them or bake them. We serve soup or salads before main courses such as steak and potatoes, not after; and we generally have something sweet for "dessert" not something sour, and not soup. In China, meals often end with soup. We generally have, codified in cookbooks and foodie magazines, a comprehensive plan for cooking foods and planning meals each day, which nobody thinks twice about. My use of cookbooks suggests another aspect of codes—they are communicated.

Codes are communicated.

All of the points I have been making about codes are implicit in the definition of codes, and so is the notion of communication as being central to codes. Much of this communication is to our unconscious. That is, we are not aware that we have learned a code. In the case of laws, we are aware of them, and, in fact, we are taught that "ignorance of the law is no excuse." But much learning is done automatically or by osmosis, so to speak. We read menus and restaurants and learn what foods go with what other foods.

A great deal of research in mass communications work is involved in searching for clues—what George Gerbner calls "cultural indicators"—to codes and to reconstituting the codes from bits and pieces that become unmasked and are revealed as existing and as affecting people. Content analysis, for example, is a very explicit attempt to find codes by searching for hidden patterns that exist in the material being studied. In a famous study of biographies in mass magazines, Leo Lowenthal discovered that magazines in the thirties and forties had biographies of heroes of production; in later years the biographies were about celebrities and movie stars, heroes of consumption.

All kinds of communication (language, gesture, music, painting and whatever kind you can think of) have a relation to the culture in which they are found; they mediate between the codes and the individual, and that code is something that can be searched for and hopefully discovered—at least in part. These communications involve such matters as assumptions people have, their values, their logic, their superstitions, their myths and legends, their "high culture" and their "popular culture." It may very well be that different disciplines, like the blind men and the elephant, spend their time with discipline specific aspects of a code or codes, and the movement for inter-disciplinary studies represents an attempt, not fully realized or understood, to crack as much of the code as is possible.

Umberto Eco, an Italian semiotician, has suggested that there is a problem with the mass media in that the codes of the creators of texts are different from the codes of the receivers of these texts, which leads to audiences not decoding the texts correctly—that is, the way the creators of the texts thought they would be understood. This suggests that large numbers of people are misinterpreting the texts they receive from the mass media because of differences in socio-economic status, education and culture. As he writes (1972):

> Codes and subcodes are applied to the message in the light of a general framework of cultural references, which constitute the receiver's patrimony of knowledge, his ideological, ethical, religious standpoints, his psychological attitudes, his tastes, his value systems, etc. (page 115)

Thus, aberrant decoding becomes the norm thanks to the mass media. We are left with the notion that audiences interpret all texts different ways and usually different from the way the creators of these texts thought they would be interpreted.

*   *   *

I have not said anything about two other important matters—how cultures are created and how they might be classified, and I do not intend to do much with either problem. It seems likely that cultures are the result of chance and circumstance; historical accidents (wars, migrations, and disasters) lead to the dominance of certain values which then become institutionalized and affect other institutions, which then reinforce the original values. This, at least is what the great German sociologist Max Weber postulated. Marxists, on the other hand, derive culture from a given system of economic relations in a country. The mode of production "determines" (in ways that are not always quite clear) the culture, which is an epiphenomenon. The problem with Marxist analyses of culture is that countries with similar modes of production and levels of economic development do not necessarily have similar cultures and value-systems. In fact they frequently have conflicting ones.

It is more important, I think, to pay attention to how cultures and *culture codes* affect people rather than speculate about the origins of cultures. We can see how particular cultures influence individuals and decide whether modifications are desirable.

Classifying cultures is another difficult problem we face in dealing with codes. Cultures are not identifiable with societies or nations; in some cases culture is broader than nations and in others much smaller. Also, there may be all kinds of mixtures of cultures and subcultures within a given geographical area. For example, there may be an American code, which refers to certain general things people in America have in common.   This would be at a very high level of abstraction.   There may also be, within that general frame of reference, regional codes such as western American culture—a regional code—that people in certain states have in common. Also, there may be a North Californian code, which, in turn, is broken up by class divisions—upper class, middle class, working class, and so forth. And, in addition, within the Northern Californian code there may exist numerous sub-cultures and counter-cultures. All of this makes generalizing about American culture or any culture or country difficult (except in very broad terms).

To see a world in a grain of sand

and a heaven in a wild flower.

To hold infinity in the palm of your hand

and eternity in an hour.

>William Blake

All Nature is but Art, unknown to thee;
All chance, direction, which thou canst not see
All discord, harmony not understood,
All partial evil, universal good:
And, spite of pride, in erring reason's spite,
One truth is clear, whatever is, is right.

>Alexander Pope, "Essay on Man"

Chapter Two

On Structures and Codes

We have just seen why it is that culture codes are so invisible. It is because they are so ubiquitous, so all-pervasive. We absorb these codes without recognizing we have done so in countless cases. For example, it has been demonstrated that the average American has an "invisible wall" about eighteen inches from his body that he regards (without knowing it) as inviolable, and if this wall is penetrated, he will do something to regain the eighteen inches of personal territory. A film called "Invisible Walls" demonstrates this over and over again, yet it is most likely that if you were to ask people about this wall they would not know what you are talking about.

Our sense of space is culture-coded like so many other things. In other cultures people have live much closer to their walls or further away from them and have different notions of privacy and related matters. As you can well imagine, when people from two cultures with different "invisible wall" distances confront one another, the situation can be most confusing. If a young Italian male, and the code in Italy is that people speak close to one another, were to engage a young American female in a conversation at a cocktail party, where the code is people speak an arm's length away from others, each would be trying to adjust the space between one another and, unknowingly, would be violating one another's sense of correctness. To the American girl, the Italian would seem forward; to the Italian, the girl would seem stand-offish.

If we accept the notion that many phenomena in our daily life have a structure and wish to search for these "secret structures," there are certain notions we must keep in mind. Here I am drawing upon the work of Lévi-Strauss, the distinguished French structuralist anthropologist, and a number of other scholars and writers who call themselves semioticians.

What Are Structures?

Structures consist of elements organized in certain ways. So our first problem is what are the elements or units we are concerned with? For example, a meal, if looked upon structurally, would consist of elements such as "sour," "sweet," "cooked," "raw," or combinations of colors or shapes. A structuralist analysis of a dinner of roast beef, roast potatoes, peas, salad, ice cream, and coffee would not be interested in the roast beef as roast beef, but rather as something "cooked" rather than being raw, or "round" or "red." It is not easy to identify minimal units or basic elements. Physicists may be able to identify the most basic element in the universe, but structuralists have to solve this problem for each topic they deal with.

How are the elements organized?

What are the rules which govern their relations? What are the rules which govern transformations? In certain cuisines the "law of opposites" may be the law of organization. Sweets are to be balanced by sours, solids by liquids, hot by cold, and so on. In some cuisines the code is every meal should contain something sweet, sour, bitter, bland, etc. Quite likely we pay no conscious attention to such matters when we eat or decide what to eat, but that is because the code for what constitutes a good breakfast, lunch or dinner is already deeply imbedded in our minds; so deeply that we are unaware of making choices on the basis of a system of selection. In the case of Army insignia another rule is at work—addition of stripes, up to a point: one stripe means private, two stripes means corporal, three stripes means sergeant. Then other rules start operating for lieutenants, captains, and so on.

What do we focus on?

Our concern is with "complex" phenomena and systems, not units. It stands to reason that if we are going to determine how a number of elements are structurally arranged, we must have more than one element or more than one item. In other words, we are dealing with cultural phenomena that are sufficiently complicated so we can detect their coding. This does *not* mean we only deal with highly involved matters, of great complexity. It merely means we cannot subject *exceedingly* simple, unitary phenomena to this kind of analysis A cup of black coffee does not yield easily to structural analysis; a complete meal does.

When I said our concern is with *systems* I used the term in

a rather general way. We can consider food as a system, fashion as a system; the term *system* refers, as I define it, to a collection of entities with a structure, with specific relations between units and with conventions that govern these relations. It means that there is a code to be discovered and that what might seem to be random and arbitrary is, in fact, governed by laws.

Smoking as a Ritual

Let us consider how seemingly simple activities are, in reality, quite complex and involved. We will take, for the object of our analysis, a very common activity, or, as we shall see, series of activities—the smoking of a cigarette. It is something hundreds of millions of people do every day for a wide variety of reasons, yet, like so much in everyday life, with very little thought to what they are doing and how they are doing it. From our point of view, smoking is a ritualized activity composed of a number of smaller acts which are the fundamental units of the ritual.

We will start by breaking the activity up into its fundamental acts. What I am doing is listing each act in a typical process known as "having a smoke" or "smoking." The acts are listed in order of occurrence:

1. taking a pack of cigarettes
2. opening it

3. selecting a cigarette
4. putting a cigarette in the mouth
5. returning pack to pocket or purse
6. taking a lighter or packet of matches
7. lighting the cigarette—puffing to start tobacco burning
8. returning the lighter to pocket or purse
9. puffing on cigarette
10. taking the cigarette out of one's mouth to exhale, flick ashes, etc.
11. grinding out the butt in an ashtray or flicking the butt away.

There are nearly a dozen micro-acts involved in smoking a cigarette. These acts can be subsumed under four different categories: *selecting*, *lighting*, *smoking* and *disposing*. The actual smoking of a cigarette occurs at the end of a relatively long sequence of acts which leads to the consumption of the cigarette, and it is all these little acts which give the smoking of cigarettes gratifications beyond that of puffing away on burning tobacco and getting a nicotine fix.

Along with the acts one must go through to smoke there are various social codes connected with smoking. For example, a person smoking in company will often ask people if they would like to have one of his cigarettes. Lately, now that many smokers have been made conscious of the fact that smoking irritates people and causes cancer in non-smokers, smokers will ask if it is permissible to smoke. The rules of etiquette also suggest that men should light cigarettes for women.

The functions of smoking are numerous; it is an activity which gives people something to do with their hands to relieve boredom or anxiety, it helps confer identity, or, rather, aids in giving a person an *image*. The brand of cigarette people smoke is a "message" they make to the world about who they are and how they sees themselves. Different brands of cigarettes use advertising to cultivate different images, so people can choose from readymade images and identities by smoking a particular brand of cigarette. *Marlboro*, once a ladies cigarette, has become identified with cowboys, ruggedness, nature and that kind of thing, while *Virginia Slims* projects an image of sophisticated, adult femininity. Cigarettes may also help assuage oral needs in people and function as a kind of reverse (in that they are cancer creating) substitute for the mother's breast.

There may also be a sense of the demonic and magical, as man transforms himself into a smoke-snorting monster, dragon, etc. An examination of the four categories under which the eleven acts involved in smoking can be grouped reveals that smoking also is connected to power urges, and smoking may be a kind of power-redeeming substitute for people who, in fact, have little power. (This thesis would suggest that working-class people would be more addicted to smoking than professional people, which happens to be the case.)

The fact that all of these indications are petty and trivial is beside the point. What is revealed is that the various kinds of acts involved in smoking involve different kinds of power: decision-making, summoning fire (a kind of magic), destroying or wasting conspicuously, and relegating to the ash heap. If we adopt the dramatic metaphor and see our actions as a kind of "theatre," in which we are the heroes (or, at least the leading men and women), smoking can be likened to a *performance* one puts on, involving a number of props— matches or lighters, cigarettes, ashtrays, etc. This performance involves a variety of physical actions:

1. opening
2. picking out with thumb and fingers
3. placing object to lips
4. scratching (matches) or pressing (lighter)
5. sucking
6. blowing
7. flicking
8. pressing or grinding

and all of these actions can be done in different ways, with different "styles." In addition there is the matter of where the cigarette is placed in the mouth (left side, center, right side), the angle at which it "dangles," how puffs are taken and the smoke exhaled, the length of the cigarette, its color, whether it has a filter tip or not, how the cigarette is held, and so on.

What is interesting is that smokers usually develop a routine and style of smoking and keep it for as long as they smoke, so that once the act or the performance is created, the actors keep on playing the role until they die or stop smoking. Because smoking involves so many different acts and confers, in subtle ways, so many psychic gratifications on the smoker-performer, it is hard to stop smoking. The addiction is more than physical; it is also psychological—nobody likes to leave show-biz! This analysis would indicate that in order to stop smoking, we must find substitute rituals, which allow people to "perform" and which take care of power needs they have. That is why chewing gum is so unsatisfactory. It is much too elemental and has connotations of childishness.

On the importance of binary oppositions?

The relationship which seems to be most useful and most pervasive in our thinking involves binary oppositions. By creating lists of opposites, we are frequently able to see relationships between things and relationships that ordinarily would have escaped our notice. That is, we can see the *logic of relationships*, which is another way of saying we can detect a *culture code*. Ferdinand de Saussure, one of the founding fathers of semiotics, said that concepts have no meaning in themselves; they take their meaning from their relationships in the system in which they are found. As he explained in his *Course in General Linguistics* (1915/1966), "Concepts are purely differential and defined not by their positive content but negatively by their relations with other terms of the system." (page 117). The most important aspect of concepts, he added, "is in being what the others are not." (page 117). Thus, for Saussure, "Signs function, then, not through their intrinsic values but through their relative position" (page 118).

A Comparison of Two Films

As an example, let us consider an analysis made of a Japanese film, *The Seven Samurai* and an American film, *The Magnificent Seven*. Robert Lifton, a well known psychiatrist, wrote his essay, "Who Is More Dry?" about contemporary Japanese youth and their values, which are mirrored in the two films—the original Japanese film (which reflects traditional

Japanese values and codes) and the American imitation (which reflects American values and codes). This chart shows how binary opposition works.

DRY	WET
The Magnificent Seven	*The Seven Samurai*
direct	evasive
logical	polite
to the point	sentimental
pragmatic	nostalgic
casual	romantic causes
self-interested	obligated to society
sunlight	cherry blossoms
jazz	moon viewing
Hemingway	Haiku
cowboys, gunmen	samurai

The oppositions here are not always perfect, but the two lists do show fundamentally different patterns—dryness and wetness, self-interest and obligation to society, cowboys and samurai. What Lifton has done for entire societies, through an analysis of two films, can be done for smaller entities and other things, like foods and fashions and formulas in popular culture, to name a few topics.

What messages are hidden in signs and symbols?

In addition to our search for *culture codes* or secret structures, we must also be on the lookout for messages hidden in symbols and signs--messages in objects of everyday life, as well as in forms of communication where it is understood that there is meaning. It is useful now to learn something more about semiotics, the science of signs. In Saussure's book, *Course in General Linguistics,* he explains the way he uses signs: He writes:

> I call the combination of a concept and a sound-image a *sign,* but in current usage the term generally designates only a sound-image, a word, for example ... I propose to retain the word *sign [signe]* to designate the whole and to replace *concept* and *sound-image* respectively by *signified [signifié]* and *signifier [signifiant];* the last two terms have the advantage of indicating the opposition

that separates them from each other and from the whole of which they are parts. As regards *sign,* if I am satisfied with it, this is simply because I do not know of any word to replace it, the ordinary language suggesting no other. (page. 67)

Every sign has two parts to it, then: a sound or image and the concept it generates. The relation between the signifier and the signified is arbitrary, based on convention. For Saussure, symbols were different. As he explained (1915/1966):

> One characteristic of the symbol is that it is never wholly arbitrary; it is not empty, for there is a rudiment of a natural bond between signifier and signified. The symbol of justice, a pair of scales, could not be replaced by just another symbol, such as a chariot. (page 68)

Semioticians debate this understanding of a symbol, but this controversy is not of great importance to our concerns. What is important is that we recognize that signs and symbols play an important role in our everyday lives.

A *sign* is also commonly defined as "a mark having a conventional meaning and used in place of words to represent a complex notion." Another definition, derived from the semiotician Umberto Eco, defines a sign as "anything that can be used to stand for something else." A *symbol*, on the other hand, can be defined as "an act, sound or object having cultural significance and the capacity to excite or objectify a response," or "an object or act that represents a repressed complex through unconscious association." It is this "unconscious" significance that is often critical, and it is our task to examine symbols in terms of their significance to our unconscious, and by extension, their influence upon our ideas and activities.

Symbols often have camouflaged meanings in a large number of cases—meanings that are not obvious to many people. There are some objects which are specifically symbols, such as a crucifix. The cross is the *signifier* and Christ, Christianity and a score of other meanings are what is *signified.* But in many cases ordinary objects have a covert symbolic dimension and we must be alert to what it is they signify.

Cocktail Signs

On a very simple level, a neon sign showing a martini glass and a stirring rod is a signifier. It signifies a bar or some kind of a place to purchase drinks. In this case the meaning is social. We learn to equate the sign with its signified, "drink purchasing," and are aware of what is signified. But in many cases we are not aware of the meaning of what is signified, by objects that are part of our experience, especially when they are not signs but rather symbols.

I would suggest, drawing upon Freudian theory, that the signs showing a cocktail (in slang, "cock" is penis and "tail" is a woman) and a swizzle stick can also be seen as a message to our unconscious--a representation of a penis pointed at a vagina. People who see these signs do not recognize the hidden meaning of these signs just as they do not recognize the codes that shape their behavior. But most people do know that alcohol decreases inhibitions and there is often a connection between drinking alcoholic beverages and having sex.

The Big Mac

The cultural "meaning" of the "Big Mac" has to be pointed out; one must explain how it is a symbol of the fast food industry, of the industrialization of eating, of massification, of unhealthy food that contributes to the obesity problem in the United States and many other countries, and, for many critics, of alienation. In 1964 I wrote an article "The Evangelical Hamburger" for *The Minnesota Daily* that argued that McDonald's had the same dynamics of evangelical religions and would soon take over the world. At the time I didn't realize that the lowly hamburger would lead to terrible medical problems and that fast food would contribute to the epidemic of diabetes in the United States and other countries

My analysis of cocktail signs and the Big Mac suggests that in many cases symbols must be interpreted and their meaning discerned, but this does not mean that the analysis can be arbitrary; that is not the case. There must be something in the logic of the situation that enables you to suggest that your analysis is not pure invention. Frequently we must combine our interest in *culture codes* and in symbols and signs, and examine the laws of combination and relations involved in systems of symbols and signs.

There is a logic to many systems of signs and other phenomena that we generally overlook. In the case of military insignia, rank is evident by the signs military people wear, but there are other areas in which a structural-semiotic analysis of signs reveals hidden things and may have considerable payoff. Recall the Saussure suggested that the meaning of symbols is not completely arbitrary.

We know there is a coded structure, of some kind, with military insignia, but there may be important areas where the structures are much more secret—fairy tales and myths, cuisines, style systems, our personalities, etc. In such areas a recognition that there are codes is vital if changes are to be made; for example, if certain kinds of neuroses are residues or consequences of a certain kind of codings, then changes may be contingent upon uncovering these codes and modifying them in various ways.

It has been suggested by Karen Horney, for example, that neurotic anxiety may be the consequence of two competing value orientations which are both important in American culture. Our economic system stresses individualism and self-interest and our religious institutions stress cooperation and love of one another. Since these two "codes" are contradictory, a person who believes in both of them will be hard pressed to observe them and will feel guilty about any violations of either code. In such a case it seems logical that something must be done on the "structural" level, and either the economic or religious codes must be modified. The political sociologist Seymour Martin Lipset argued, in his book *The First New Nation,* that Americans were torn between two other dominant values—achievement and equality, which are in continual conflict with one another. It is somewhat of a simplification, but it would seem that the Republican party stresses achievement (and the "liberty" needed to implement this value) and the Democratic party stresses equality and the laws needed to support this value.

The problem of neurotic anxiety points to a difficulty people face. How do they reconcile conflicting codes? There seem to be two ways out. Individuals can split themselves up into two, dissociated selves, and be Christian on Sundays and businessmen the rest of the week to carry on with the problem at hand. Or people can reject the general values of the culture and become anomic (meaning "against the norms" literally), either identifying with, or joining, sub-cultures whose value orientations (codes) are not completely congruent with the culture at large, (Generally speaking political groups in America center on different codes, which explains the two ideological positions here: liberal and conservative or Democrat and Republican, discussed above.) We must keep in mind then that frequently there is the problem of competing and conflicting codes to be dealt with in our societies and cultures.

The question of the reality of codes is also of interest. Are there codes buried in folklore, cuisines and other phenomena, or are these codes that I and others have found clever constructions imposed on the material being studied. That is, is there a "design within," or is the design in the mind of the person who more or less invents it. Are *culture codes* imbedded in the phenomena we study or are they figments of our (my?) imagination? Do we *find* them or do we *fabricate* them?   This problem is sometimes described as "God's Truth versus Hocus Pocus." Personally speaking, I believe we find what is already there—though I don't know how I can prove this all the time.

This matter of the reality of *culture codes* is connected to the reality of culture itself. This is a subject of considerable controversy. In brief, there is a controversy between those anthropologists who believe that culture is merely an abstraction used to characterize a number of different activities of man and those who believe these activities are, in themselves, culturological and culture really exists. As Leslie A. White says in *The Concept of Culture* (Burgess Publishing Company) "…the conception of culture subscribed to here, namely the Tylorian conception, is that culture consists of real things and events to start with." (page 34.)

The matter of whether culture is "real" or not, and whether *culture codes* exist or are created in the minds of anthropologists and social-scientists is not terribly important for our purposes, and I raised it merely to indicate that it is a problem that exists. Since I have defined culture as being codes that have a secret structure, the reality or non-reality of culture must be, at the least, considered. But I think it is much more important to examine our culture in terms of its codes and secret structures and see what we find than argue about culture theory.

There are a few other considerations I should like to deal with before looking at some of the manifestations of *culture codes*. In the preceding section on the characteristics of *culture codes*, I listed the qualities they have that make them invisible—such things as concreteness, coherence, clarity, comprehensiveness, and so forth. All of these characteristics must be operative for the codes to remain unnoticed, so it is important that the codes have these characteristics. If they do not, they no longer channel behavior from the shadows, so to speak, but rather become social problems. When this happens they are subject to decision-making and rational choice, and the codes move from the realm of culture to the realm of society and politics. That is, they become rules, regulations, laws, etc.

There are two perspectives for considering the function of *culture codes*: we can examine them in terms of how they affect individuals whose behavior is guided or "shaped" by them, and we can examine them in terms of their utility to social scientists. *Culture codes* serve individuals by enabling them to fit into society and other groupings (or sub-groupings). The codes tell you what to do and how to do it. That is, they help socialize people, and the invisibility of the *culture codes* is connected to their efficacy. The more they form what people "take for granted" or "that which goes without saying," the more powerful they are and the less we take notice of them.

For the social scientist, on the other hand, the codes are extremely useful in that they enable us to predict behavior. It is their structure that makes prediction possible. If the *culture codes* are operating smoothly we can generally tell how a person will act in a given situation. Let me cite an example drawn from the military, though the example involves rules and not *culture codes.* The rule is that enlisted men salute only officers and not other enlisted men, and vice-versa. We are dealing here with the code of exclusion.

To see how a knowledge of *culture codes* helps make predictions, let us return to the subject of food. Supposing I were to ask an American the following question, "What goes with a broiled porterhouse steak?" I asked some of my friends and most of them said "baked potato, of course." Some said French Fries. Then they list such dishes as salad, green beans (and decidedly not peas) or creamed spinach, and several other items. We have laws of combination in foods which are extremely powerful, though we seldom think of them. And once we choose our main dish, the side dishes almost suggest themselves. Consider our options once we decide to eat a steak:

Food	Porterhouse steak.
Cooking	Broil, grill
Side Dishes	Salad and cooked green vegetable
Starch	Baked potato or French fries

This combination of steak and baked potato or French fries or, possibly, roast potatoes, is an American one; in France there would be a different cut of steak and the French would almost always have what we call "French fries" (pommes frites) with it. Some Americans would eat catsup with their steaks, an idea horrible to the French. Many French people would eat mustard with their steak, an idea horrible to the Americans. The point is, then, that some combinations may exist across a spectrum of cultures, and others may be more or less unique to one. In addition, there are codes about how long the steak should be cooked: medium rare (when the flesh is all pink) tends to be the standard, but some people like their stakes rare or very rare. These notions about how long steak should be cooked are shaped, in large part, by socio-economic status.

In the next chapter I will take the notion of *culture codes* and use it to deal with a wide variety of sociological concepts. For example, I will use *culture codes* to examine identity, social roles, institutions, ideologies, and cultural phenomena such as rituals, folktales, and systems such as cuisines and fashion. We can see how these subjects relate to academic disciplines in the following chart:

Discipline	Manifestation
Psychology	Identity
Social Psychology	Social Roles
Sociology	Institutions
Political Science	Ideologies
Anthropology	Rituals

One last point: when we talk about codes we often mean they are ways of disguising messages. What is the message we get from our examination of *culture codes*? I would say it is human behavior that is the message and it is the codes which help us to understand this behavior. Fashion, cuisine, and other "systems" are programs of behavior informed by a secret structure or codes, and when we discover the codes we discover their roots of action.

"And someone, I can't recall who, mentioned that you have a fascinating theory about identity—namely that we're all impostors, or something like that."
Duerfklein laughed.
"Yes, impostors!   That's the word.   My theories really bother my colleagues because they tend to look at human beings in aggregates, as members of society or some class or culture or sub-culture. So they can talk about things like behavior in crowds or American identity—whatever that might be—or various ideological positions, that still deal with large groups of people—women, gays, people of color, the proletariat. You name it. My focus, since I have a psychoanalytic approach to things, deals with individuals and how they achieve their identities. Or don't achieve them, since many people, as my theory suggests, are pretenders to an identity.... You must remember that the term 'personality' is based on the Latin root 'persona' which means mask. So our personalities are, it can be said, masks that we create to deal with others in social situations. You might contrast one's personality with what might be called one's character or 'self,' one's true being. What I argue, based on my work with numerous patients, is that many people never grow up, never cast off immature notions and fantasies of what it means to be an adult, never achieve coherence and continuity in their sense of themselves, so what you get, ultimately, is a fake person, a simulation, a fraud. And these people can't help themselves because they don't even recognize that they are impostors. They've devoted all their energy to fooling others and they end up also fooling themselves."
Arthur Asa Berger, *Mistake in Identity*

Chapter Three

Codes and Human Behavior

Let me now use the concept of codes to
investigate a number of topics of interest to
scholars. I begin with identity.

Personal Identity as a Code
Identity is now one of the major problems of the age. The fact
that so many people are unsure of their identities and insecure
about themselves (or is it *their* selves?) is an indictment of the
age and our societies. In the middle ages, when there was a
wholeness to life and a grand synthesis, when everyone had a
place in the great chain of being, identity was not a problem.
Saving one's soul—and frequently one's body—was! Now
that most of us have physical security we find ourselves
plagued with other problems and anxieties, and of these, the
question of our identities is now paramount. We smashed the
chains, which tied us together in the middle ages and find
ourselves tied by chains we cannot seem to elude. For, among
other things, our freedom has meant freedom to doubt our
identities.

The word *identity* comes from the Latin *identitat*,
which means "the same as" and from *identidem*, which means
"repeatedly." *The Random House Unabridged Dictionary*
defines identity as "state or fact of remaining the same one, as

under varying aspects or conditions," and as "the condition of being oneself or itself and not another."

The key notion is *continuity.* If we take the two Latin meanings and join them together we get "repeatedly the same as," and this is what we generally mean when we use the term *identity*. Our bodies change, the situations in which we find ourselves change, the societies about us change, but there is this *constant* behind the changing situations and roles which we each identify as our "self" and which is our identity. If we return to our notion of *culture codes*, we can see that the idea of coherent structure fits in here. An identity is a personal code, a distinctive way of combining elements leading to something unique. If there is no coherence and no continuity there is no identity, there is nothing to talk about, except, perhaps, the different changes in a person and what generated them..

There are, however, people who take constant change as the unifying aspect of their personalities. They are *chameleons*, who take on colorations from their surroundings. Their particular "constant" is constant change and the negation of a coherent self. It is an unsatisfactory identity because it has no internal structure and defines itself only in terms of relations to outside factors. In postmodern societies, identity as a "coherent sense of self" is of no great concern; people change their identities often, because in societies where the grand narratives have been rejected, societies described by the French scholar Jean Francois Lyotard as having "incredulity toward metanarratives," we face a crisis of legitimation and anything goes.

One of the reasons it is so difficult to discuss identity is because there are several other terms, namely *character* and *personality* that keep intruding (as it were) into the subject. Is a person's character the same as his identity? Is one's personality one's identity? And is character the same as personality?

It is easiest to work backwards here. The word *personality* has as its stem *persona*, which means "mask." A personality then can be looked upon as a *mask* which we use in order to hide our true selves from others—and perhaps ourselves. It is a projection, a creation, something which may be false, something very artificial. Yet it is frequently used as a way of describing an individual. When we ask about someone's personality we want to know "What is he like?" and "Who is she?"

Actually, though, we often use the word personality when we *mean* in fact character and we use both when we mean identity. Character means a person's attributes and distinctive qualities, amongst other things. (*The Random House Dictionary* lists 28 different meanings for the term and suggests that ethical standards and moral qualities belong to character, while personality involves "outer and inner characteristics that determine the impression which one makes on others.") I would suggest that character and personality are both manifestations of something more fundamental, namely identity. I use the term character for the moral realm and the term personality for the social realm.

Identity, Character and Personality
The terms are used in different ways by different people and loosely by almost everyone. The chart above suggests one way of understanding the way they relate to one another. According to this schema, character and personality are aspects of something more fundamental—namely identity. Character and personality must also have continuity to be meaningful. The question people ask themselves when they question their identities, "Who am I?" can be restated in another, more meaningful way: How am I different from others? For, if people are not distinctive and different from others, in some ways, we can question whether they have a personal identity.

It is useful if we think of another way of defining identity that may be helpful here. Suppose we break up the word *identity* somewhat differently than is traditionally done and obtain two segments: one comprising the term "id" and the other the term "entity." If we think of the "id" in terms of the Greek *idios* rather than the Latin *idens* we get a slightly different notion of identity, since *idios* means private, personal, separate, distinct, own. (An idiot is a "completely private person," and our understanding of the word identity is closer to the word *idiosyncratic*, though without the negative associations.)

This leads us to redefine identity in terms of a private thing, a personal or distinctive thing, our own thing. People who use the phrase, "do my own thing," are really, without knowing it, asserting their right to act in congruence with their perceived identities. This leads to a problem: What happens when doing one's "own thing" interferes with someone else's "thing" or rights? The right of a person to do his "own thing" implies the right of everyone to do his "own thing," and when there is a collision it is very difficult to resolve, if doing one's "own thing" is the only criterion.

With this new definition or understanding of identity in mind, we can look at the problem posed above: In what ways is anyone distinctive, does anyone have a personal, unique identity? I would make a distinction between two radically opposed kinds of identities—what I call the *anonymous* identity and what I call the *authentic* identity. To see the differences between these orientations examine the chart which follows:

Anonymous Identity	Authentic Identity
Extrinsically shaped	Intrinsically shaped
Externally manipulated	Internally directed
Mediated (shaped by media)	Self-organized
Transparent	Substantive
Chaotic	Integrated
No Self	Self
Impostor	Real identity
Common	Personal

Anonymous and Authentic Identities

The items on the left, under the Anonymous Identity, all suggest randomness, haphazardness, falseness, lack of coherence. A person who is anonymous, that is without a name or without individuality, feels himself to be a creation of external forces, a kind of fictitious entity, who has been overwhelmed by mass society and the mass media. He creates himself in different *images*, but there is no relation between his image and his self, for he does not know his self. The images could have been quite different, for there is no necessity behind one or another. In my mystery novel, *Mistake in Identity,* I call these people "impostors."

He or she presents to the world a collection of pseudo-selves or impostor selves which change with the dictates of the fashion world and media. This may be because he cannot get in touch with his true self, or will not, preferring to keep it submerged as a way of avoiding pain. The price is a loss of strong feelings and of a sense of self; in short, anonymity. Jean Francois Lyotard offers an example of this kind of person in his book *The Postmodern Condition: A Report on Knowledge.* He writes (1984:76):

> Eclecticism is the degree zero of contemporary general culture: one listens to reggae, watches a western, eats McDonald's food for lunch and local cuisine for dinner, wears Paris perfume in Tokyo and "retro" clothes in Hong Kong; knowledge is a matter for TV games. It is easy to find a public for eclectic works. By becoming kitsch, art panders to the confusions which reigns in the "taste" of patrons. Artists, gallery owners, critics and the public wallow together in the "anything goes," and the epoch is one of slackening.

In postmodern societies, like the United States and many other advanced societies, one plays around with one's identity at will. The only cost is the money needed to purchase the right clothes and accessories or take trips to the right places.

Although we have made some progress in understanding identity, I feel there are further clarifications to be made, which will, in fact, lead up to modify our notion of what identity is. There are several reasons for my feeling this way. First, we have not said anything about *personal history* or biography. It seems to me that a person's unique history, and we all have unique histories, has a great deal of influence upon a person's identity. It may be, of course, that our personalities shape our histories and experiences in great measure, though that raises the question of how we arrived at our personalities. In any case, along with character and personality, I think we must consider biography as a fundamental constituent of identity.

There is also the problem of whether identity is personal and private, public, or both. For example, in David Karp's nightmarish dystopia, *One*, the hero is completely re-identified, via drug treatment, etc. He is given a new name, a new (and fabricated) biography, a new job, new friends— every social aspect of his identity is changed, and yet he himself *is not changed,* and ultimately must be destroyed. His destruction is, it turns out, his triumph, for the fact that he must be destroyed means that the dystopia in which he lived cannot survive because it cannot completely change people; there is something within them that resists all the techniques of persuasion, manipulation, and re-identification that the state can utilize.

This particular example raises an important question. Is identity merely a collection of demographic and psychographic categories applied to people: race, religion, education, sex, age, occupation, ethnic background, nationality, social class, etc., or is it that, as well as character, personality, and biography? The solution to this problem may be in dividing identity up into two spheres: the public or social, in which a person is "defined" as a collection of psychographic and demographic categories; and private identity, in which a person's character, personality, and biography are the dominant factors. We can split identity up into two parts: *social* identity and *ego* or *personal* identity.

If Americans define themselves as seeing themselves as having escaped from history and as Adamic innocents with no past, it means that the vital historic dimension is lacking, so that identity is a problem for all Americans, since they cannot rely upon a tangible, solid, historical background to tell them who they are. *Escaping from history also means escaping from a secure identity; this escapism leads to anxiety conspicuous consumption, compulsive other-directedness and a host of other plagues.* Nobody knows who he is, so everyone imitates everyone else. Thus, ironically, the lack of a historic identity, the lack of tradition, means that people conform more readily to norms picked up from popular culture and other institutions in our mass society.

We escaped from history to become prisoners of the latest fad, prisoners of the moment, of the media, of the present. Americans have not realized that another word for rejection of the past, history and tradition is *amnesia;* and we tend to suffer from a cultural amnesia that troubles us sorely. The problem of the amnesiac is, after all, that of identity. Who am I? amnesiacs ask, since they cannot remember their past; and we, as a nation, have, in essence, the same problem. This matter is important to people because national identity—being an American or a Frenchman, for instance—plays a significant role in their individual identities. We are social animals, and the social ambiance in which we grow up plays a major role in our identity-formation. That is, our culture shapes us to a greater extent than we generally recognize—viz. the matter of invisible walls and attitudes towards space and many other attitudes and tastes we have. In the case of Americans, the fact that we have (as a society) defined ourselves as having escaped from the past, from history, means that each individual in America has the task of creating anew his own identity—within the parameters, that is, allowed by his culture.

I have suggested in various writings that we Americans see ourselves as *spiritual* orphans, and this concept affects us all as individuals. In the comics we had *Little Orphan Annie* and *Superman* both of whom were orphans, and our popular literature was full of orphans who, one way or another, succeeded in the world. This idea (which is a social one) influences the way we relate to our parents and our children. We feel we've been abandoned by our parents or, at least, our fatherlands, and our children actually leave home as soon as they are able, by running away, by early marriage, or some other arrangement), and their parents can hardly wait for them to go. (A study has found that Americans are happiest before they have children and after their children have left home.) The economic problems of recent years means we now have many "boomerang children," young men and women, of college age and sometime older, returning to live with their parents because they can't afford to live on their own.

Transactional psychologists frequently talk about "scripts" which children pick up, essentially from their parents. By the time the average child is three or six, depending upon which psychologist you read, the child has a sense of himself and a way of relating to the world that is more or less fixed. And this script will determine how he or she relates to other people and lives his or her life. I would suggest another word for script would be *code, a list of internalized, unrecognized (but potent) rules for behavior which shapes actions.* (NOTE: recent research suggests that during adolescence people have a chance to modify their scripts and acquire new ones. But the importance of our first years of life in shaping us is very great.)

Code is a better word than script, I feel, because it is more general, though script is useful because it suggests a person is an actor whose lines have been given him. If we return to our earlier definition of *culture codes* we gain an interesting insight. I defined these *culture codes* as "secret structures which shape our behavior," which means they are the same thing (on the personal level) as scripts. They have the same function, though codes are general as well as personal.

It seems, then, that we can define personal identity as a private code or a private version or adaptation of a general code which we adopt, generally without recognizing we have done so, and which then affects our subsequent behavior. Identity, then, has two dimensions: a personal one, which involves character, personality and biography, as well as the "private codes" an individual picks up; and a social one, which is the demographic and psychographic categories and classifications that people use to "identify" a person—age, sex, generation, religion, occupation, friendly, affectionate, and so on. Let us reformulate our chart on relationships involved in identity:

Personal Aspects	Social Aspects
Ego Identity	Group Identity
Personality	Character
History	Self

Personal and Social Aspects of Identity

This chart shows that identity has two dimensions: the social aspect refers to our membership in various "categories" which enable other people to place us in some kind of a niche, and the personal aspect refers to our personal history, self and moral point of view.

We can test the usefulness of this chart by taking the problem of amnesia into consideration. From the point of view of another person, if we know the various social categories by which we can classify a person we have a pretty good idea of his identity. If we know him and have an idea of his personality, we believe we have even a better idea. Actually, the social categories give a capsule view of a person's biography, a kind of social, categorical biography. What an amnesiac loses is his biography, his personal history. He maintains everything else, but the loss of a personal history is so great that the amnesiac as, in effect, lost his identity.

Social Roles as Identity Codes

If identity is a personal or private code, social roles are identity codes for public situations. A role is commonly defined as the way a person acts in a given social situation, though it is much more complex than that. Ralph Turner, in the *International Encyclopedia of the Social Sciences*, defines a *role* as having the following elements:

> It provides a comprehensive p*attern* for behavior and attitudes; it constitutes a *strategy* for coping with a recurrent type of situation; it is *socially identified*, more or less clearly, as an entity; it is subject to being played recognizably by *different individuals;* and it supplies a major basis for *identifying* and *placing* persons in society.

The terms "strategy" and "pattern" suggest codes and policies on the part of the actor or person playing the role. (We use the term actor not in terms of its theatrical definition but sociologically, to refer to a person who plays roles in social interactions, not in theatrical productions. Of course the term role suggests that all our social relationships have this element of drama in them, and the use of theatre as a metaphor has been an important development in social thought in recent years.)

The remainder of Turner's definition deals with the other party or parties involved, the "audience" for the role player. The audience must know the code or they will not be able to respond properly to the role. They will not understand what is being communicated, and that will lead to a great deal of confusion. The fact that others can assume a role only serves to illustrate the difference between an identity and a role. Roles can be assumed by anyone, though the roles a person plays are a function of his identity. Our roles are tied to the expectations of others who have notions about how a given role is to be played. They, in turn, have *counter-roles* which allow for the enactment of a role.

The very notion of a role suggests communication and response—communication to others and response by others—and roles can only be played out when there are others who enable a person to play a role. If we look upon life as being somewhat like a play, we see that our roles are contingent upon other people playing counter-roles (from our perspective these roles are counter-roles; from their perspective our roles are counter-roles) and confirming us in our roles, and vice versa. Roles, then, can only be played when other people know how the role is to be played and what the proper responses are in given situations—in short, when people understand the rules of the game, or the code. Let us look at the role of the prostitute, an example that is frequently cited in discussions of roles. Prostitutes exist in a web of relationships or counter-roles with police, Johns, pimps, lawyers, colleagues, and so on.

Roles and Counter Roles

In this particular situation, we have designated the prostitute as playing the central role and listed some of the other counter-roles which revolve around her and which are necessary for the role; that is, the people playing the counter-roles could be looked upon, here, as the "rest of the cast." They support the lead actress—the prostitute—and enable her to play her role. They also interact in various situations (pimp and customer, pimp and police, lawyer and police) and frequently help the role player learn his or her role.

It must be emphasized that a role is not an identity. For example, there are occasionally newspaper accounts about respectable housewives from suburbia who become bored and spend a few afternoons a week as prostitutes. They move from one role (loving mother, maker of sandwiches, taxi-driver for kids, etc.) to another. In the case of prostitutes (who might hope to move to the status of respectable housewives) the role becomes so dominant that it may shape the rest of their lives. The roles we play are factors in our identities, determined in large part by our status (rank) in organizations where we play our roles.

Let us now consider a person who is a college professor. Being a professor involves playing roles with others: colleagues, students, administrators, the general public, and so on. The way a people relate to others as a professor is determined by their rank; thus an assistant professor generally relates "deferentially" to associate and full professors, who have more rank than he has, relates as an equal to other assistant professors, and is superior to instructors. A professor who is a "star" or "superstar" relates differently to administrators than does an ordinary run-of-the-mill professor, and so on.

In the course of a few hours professors may take on a number of different roles, each of which is determined in part by their status and the expectations of others. Then, when they return home they play other roles, relative to their spouses, children and others. Since all role playing involves others in counter-roles, and we play many different roles in the course of a day, it means that there must be an enormous number of parts for people to learn in order for society to function smoothly.

When people do not know how to play counter-roles, there is confusion and chaos. Thus, when large numbers of so-called "disadvantaged" young people were brought into the universities, there were many problems because many of these students did not know how to relate to professors and other students according to the conventions (or codes of conduct) for students in universities. The problem these students faced was that of *socialization*—learning how to become a member of society or (in this case, of a particular institution), learning the appropriate patterns of behavior or codes. From our point of view, socialization involves *learning* and internalizing *culture codes* so people can fit into society or a group of some sort, so they can function without stress and anxiety about what is proper in a given social situation. We not only must learn these codes but we must *internalize* them, make them parts of us, take them within our psyche and adopt them as

if we had thought them up.   These roles and the attitudes relating to them became lost to our consciousness; but though we are unaware of them, they are still there, guiding us. We incorporate the codes as our own and they become part of us.

Let us return to the psychologists who have used the term

"scripts" to deal with this matter. Their argument, once again, is that at a very early age (between three and six) we are all given scripts by our parents that will determine how we function for the rest of our lives—unless there is intervention by a psychiatrist or a similar figure. The script would be a general role, such as "villain" or "sufferer" or "jerk" or "good guy" or "leader" or some other stance. That is, to continue on with the metaphor of life as a drama, we are given "character roles" and act out these roles in all situations, whenever possible, that is. These character parts are the personal side of identity (which was discussed earlier), and a role is something which mediates between our identity and a given situation. This could be diagrammed as follows:

Identity   ROLE   Situation

Our role is contingent upon two important factors: our identity (especially our status) and the situation in which we find ourselves when called upon to play our role. The importance of our scripts is that they function as codes which tell us how to play all our roles, no matter what the given situation.   The script gives security at the price of flexibility and openness to experience. And in certain cases the script is terribly destructive. Some people who have been given scripts, who have been "programmed" in terms of destructive identities and personalities, are following codes which must be discovered and changed.

There is a problem that arises here. Our identity

(especially the status we have in an organization or society in general) influences the way we play our roles, but our roles also give people an idea about our identities. Which is basic? I would say our identities, because roles are not the only factor people use in identifying people. A doctor may be a hippie, but the fact that he is a doctor—his social identity—carries more weight, in terms of how people relate to him, than his hippy identity--most of the time, that is.

The Playboy: A Case Study

Let us take the playboy for a case study. Being a playboy is a role; it may be a person's leading part and most dominant role, which colors his other roles, but it is still a role, as I see things, and not an identity. A playboy can be thought of as a well to do, carefree male who devotes most of his time to self-amusement, leisure, and various hedonistic pursuits. Playboys typically spend a great deal of time at parties and night clubs, and focus their attention on romancing a rapid succession of attractive young women.

The word "playboy" is made up of two simpler words—play and boy. *Play* suggests fun, games, lack of seriousness; and *boy* suggests immature, not adult, and perhaps even childish. A playboy, then, is someone who is always playing around, who refuses to get serious, maybe even to grow up, and become a constructive member of society. There is an element of Don Juanism to the playboy—in this role he seeks non-relational sex and is always, perhaps compulsively, involved in seeking out and conquering, to the extent he can, beautiful women. His script may have been something like "do not get involved, do not show love, lest you be hurt." Thus, all his relations are characterized by distance and manipulation.

Now the question arises—how does one get to be a playboy? It is a role that must be learned like all other roles. The way that most young men in America learn to be playboys or perhaps "pseudo-playboys" (who have the mentality but not the cash) is by reading *Playboy* and other similar magazines. The stories show the general attitude a person is to take in dealings with the other sex, and the advertisements provide a person with the correct symbol system.

A person announces to the world, and to young women in particular, that he *is* a playboy by adopting a rather limited set of symbols which serve to identify him. Thus, he finds in *Playboy* magazine a code which leads to the creation of a role—he drinks certain drinks, he drives certain cars, he buys certain clothes, he wears his hair a certain way, he has certain expectations in his relations with women, and so on. The typical playboy, if you judge him from the advertisements in *Playboy,* comes across as a bourgeois character, who might be middle or upper-middle class, but who definitely is rather conventional. He is an adaptation, for American purposes, of the classic playboy, the Latin American millionaire living off an inheritance and squandering his money chasing after beautiful women, usually in very expensive sports cars. In America, the playboy has been democratized and diluted for working class males: beer instead of champagne, Toyotas instead of Mercedes Benzes.

What is important for our purposes is that the major constituents of a playboy's roles are taken care of. Being a playboy is not necessarily a permanent role; some men are playboys when they are young, but eventually settle down and become productive members of society. And the reverse is true with a lot of men, who lead conventional lives and, suddenly, as the result of a mid-life crisis, throw it all over and become—or try to become—playboys. This is frequently called "male menopause," which hits men in their mid-fifties and sixties and sometimes later. They want to step out of one life and step into another, more exciting one. The problem is that young women see them not so much as playboys but as "dirty old men." For as we've seen, roles are contingent upon others playing counter roles which "confirm" the original roles.

Note that in the definition of role there are a number of terms that suggest codes and structure: *pattern, strategy, recurrent, socially identifiable.* All of these imply codes, leading me to suggest *that roles are codes for public situations.*

Institutions as Regulatory Coded Entities

The term "institution" is the central concept of sociology, it does not mean building, though many institutions are housed in buildings, and some, such as the military, are identified with specific buildings, namely the Pentagon. For the sociologist, institutions, such as marriage, government, and religion, provide regulatory codes for people to follow. They regulate behavior through codes or patterns which lead people to act in certain ways. Institutions are characterized by a number of attributes: they seem to have an "external reality," existing outside of people, and they usually have coercive power; that is, they can enforce their codes.

So from our perspective *an institution is a collection of codes which insure* (to the extent this is possible) *that people will act in certain ways, and will know how to act in specific situations.* The basic function of institutions is to make it possible for people to live relatively harmoniously by providing them with patterns of expected behavior (or specific roles).

In an earlier section I mentioned the problems many universities faced when disadvantaged students were admitted—students who didn't know the roles that they were expected to play and who therefore created many strains and problems. Any institution has problems when the members do not know what roles they are to play and how to play them, or will not agree on such matters. Thus the "authority" of professors depends, to a great degree, upon students accepting this authority and not challenging it—at least in the areas where the professor's role as educator is concerned.

In institutions it is a person's *position* which gives him or her authority and power. That is, the "office" in the institution is what is critical, not the personality or other characteristics of the officeholder. The institutions run on the basis of policy directives, which are promulgated from on high and which relieve members of the institution from having to make personal decisions—and from having to relate to people as individuals. Thus many institutions are run along bureaucratic lines and lead to depersonalization and de-individualization, for people are not treated as unique persons but in terms of some classification scheme.

For example, a university is an institution characterized by bureaucracy, in which administrators (who run the place but do not teach) generally set policy for professors (who teach but do not run the place to a great extent). Thus, there are codes for professors to follow which are explicitly stated, and that's what a policy is in a bureaucracy. There are also codes which are not "stated" but which exist—such as the way professors and students are to relate to one another. The main difference between what I have been calling *culture codes* and institutional policies is that policies are overt and institutions are always calling attention to their policies so everyone will know what to expect.

Policies have the characteristics of *culture codes:* that is, they must be coherent, clear, comprehensive, and all the other phenomena mentioned earlier. Some social scientists make a distinction between organizations and institutions. Thus, Melvin Tumin writes in *Patterns of Society*, a sociology textbook published a number of years ago, that an institution is "a set of tasks and patterned ways of accomplishing these tasks that are indispensable to the continuity of a society over more than one generation. Biological reproduction of the population, social and cultural transmissions of values and skills, and providing goods and services are among the basic institutions of a society." (page 422)

He differentiates these institutions from hospitals, prisons and colleges, which he describes as organizations. The difference between institutions and organizations lies in the matter of scope; institutions use organizations to do certain things, and organizations are very specific kinds of entities with policies and a much more formally elaborated code of operations than you find in social institutions. Thus education is an institution and a college is an organization. The difference between them becomes quite blurred, however, in many cases. However you care to define institution, most social scientists would agree that the notion of pattern and structure is central.

All I am suggesting is that another word for this pattern is *culture code*, and that this pattern has characteristics which I have identified as belonging to codes. Central to all of this is the matter of communication, for institutions survive and perpetuate themselves because they are able to communicate their special codes to members of society in general, or of organizations in particular.

The central phenomenon in all of what we have been talking about is the code: and identities, roles, institutions, societies and cultures are amplifications of codes, on wider and wider levels. If we visualize all this as a pyramid, identity would be on the top and culture at the base.

Identity

Institutions

Society

Culture

I assume, here, that a culture is broader than a society; it seems to me that American society is part of a general Atlantic or Euro-American culture, though many of our institutions are distinctive and our society produces a distinctive kind of modal personality in the typical American. I don't believe a culture stops at a nation's boundaries, where its political dominance ends (though not necessarily its political influence).

Socio-Economic Class as Code

It is extremely difficult making distinctions between cultures and societies and to define terms in the social sciences. For example: is an institution an organization or is it an activity? I have defined it as both, but many would not agree with me. What do we do, say, with the phenomenon of social class? It is an institution that exists in all societies with certain functions: differentiating between people, fostering certain values and attitudes, etc. Americans may share a common culture, and this sharing is in certain superficial ways made greater by the mass media—but the differences among Americans in different classes are enormous.

The late W. Lloyd Warner, a distinguished sociologist and anthropologist, suggested that there are six different classes in America: upper-upper,   lower-upper,   upper-middle, lower-middle, upper-lower, and lower-lower; the differences between these classes are so great that it is not adequate to break American society down into just three classes—upper, middle and lower.   In his classic book, *American Life*, he spelled out the different attitudes and behavior in the various classes (and frequently the difference between upper middle and lower middle class behavior is substantial) and suggested the distribution of classes in America is such that the top of the pyramid, the Upper-Uppers, are about one percent of the population and the bottom of the pyramid, the Lower-Lowers, are about twenty percent.

Though Warner wrote many years ago, his figures are still fairly representative; the modern American "welfare-warfare" state may have cut down on the number of people living in poverty, which approximates Warner's "lower-lower" level, but the gains have been minimal. In recent years, the upper-upper classes have become increasingly wealthy and the lower-lower classes have become poorer. The class makeup of American society is still close to the way he pictured it, except that inequality is growing and it is a social problem that is shaping American politics. Social class shapes people's attitudes towards toilet training, child raising, time, use of physical punishment, sexual relationships, education, food— almost everything of significance in our daily lives. Middle class people are characterized by the deferred gratification pattern (DGP). As Warner says:

> Children of the middle and upper classes are raised with their eyes on a goal of achievement for which they must, if necessary, make present sacrifices. They are expected to go to college and

to strive for high occupational status. Restraint is put on present activities for the sake of future gain. (page 88, *American Life)*

Warner describes the differences between segments of each class and the classes themselves, leading to the conclusion that there are six different class-based life-styles in American society. We might say that each of Warner's classes has a code, a set of attitudes and notions about clothes, sex, education, food, etc., which shapes the way it lives, its style of living. These life-styles (sub codes) are learned in the family and through the mass-media, two of the most fundamental socializing agencies in any society.

Social class is an institution whose function for society is quite debatable. Many social scientists point out that every society is characterized by hierarchies, in which different classes perform, for the most part, different tasks. This stratification (with different people having different statuses) is necessary, conservative social scientists suggest, because it is necessary to motivate people to fill different positions in society. Some positions require more training than others (surgeon as compared with ditch digger), are more difficult and are given more rewards, both in terms of status and salary. Otherwise, it is argued, it would be impossible to get people to defer their gratifications—to study long and hard—if they weren't given rewards for this sacrifice.

Thus, it is argued, social inequality and stratification is an unconsciously evolved institution in every society, which arises because it is necessary to get different jobs done. Inequality is all-pervasive because it is needed, so the argument goes. There is always an element of upward mobility, to keep the system going and maintain a certain amount of flexibility, but by and large, once a system of stratification is established, it tends to perpetuate itself. The top one percent in the United States is growing increasingly wealthy, thanks to the tax system.

Statistics show that the United States has less social mobility than many other countries, which means that the "American Dream," that one can rise in the world if one has enough will power and is willing to work hard, is no longer operative and no longer shapes the thinking of large numbers of Americans. Surveys reveal that many older Americans believe their children won't live as well as they live.

Stratification not only helps keep a society functioning, but it also imposes strains upon it when the poor people no longer *accept* their inferior status and insist upon a better division of the economic pie. (There are other arguments about the destructiveness of stratification which I have not cited.) From this perspective the mass media can be looked upon as a socializing institution—serving those at the top who own and control the media—for perpetuating the class system, for "brainwashing" the masses into believing that everything is as it must be. "Whatever is, is right," said Pope, a poetic spokesman for conservative thinking.

Ideologies as Socio-Political Codes.

The term *ideology* has a long history, and a confusing one. One of the biggest problems in dealing with the term is that it is used in so many different ways and means so many different things to people. One of the best definitions of the concept of ideology is found in the Introduction to Meenakshi Gigi Durham and Douglas M. Kellner's *Media and Cultural Studies: Key Works.* The write (2001):

> The concept of *ideology* forces readers to perceive that all cultural texts have the distinct biases, interests, and embedded values, reproducing the point of view of their producers and often the values of the dominant social groups. Karl Marx and Friedrich Engels coined the term "ideology" in the 1840s to describe the dominant ideas and representations in a given social order...During the capitalist era, values of individualism, profit, competition, and the market became dominant, articulating the ideology of the new bourgeois class which was consolidating its class power. Today, in our high tech and global capitalism, ideas that promote globalization, new technologies, and an unrestrained market economy are becoming the prevailing ideas—conceptions that further the interests of the new governing elites in the global economy...Ideologies appear natural, they seem to be common sense, and thus are often invisible and elude criticism. Marx and Engels began a critique of ideology, attempting to show how ruling ideas

> reproduce dominant social interests trying to naturalize, idealize, and legitimate the existing society and its institutions and values. (p. 6)

Marxist ideological analysis claims that the media and other forms of communication are used in capitalist nations, dominated by a bourgeois ruling class, to generate false consciousness in the masses, or in Marxist terms, the proletariat. We must remember that just because people are not conscious of the fact that they hold ideological beliefs does not mean they don't hold them. Most often they haven't brought their beliefs to consciousness and may not be able to articulate them.

For our purposes, what is important in this definition is the fact that ideologies are coherent socio-political programs (or codes), amongst other things. Let me now discuss one of the most influential political ideologies, Marxism. I should add that there are a many different kinds of Marxists, each of whom claims to be the true interpreter of what Marx meant. Despite the problem of different interpretations of Marx, most scholars would say that there are a set of basic beliefs and ideas which most everyone would identify as central to Marxism. Some of these would be:

The Materialist Conception of History.
Society, Marx said, determines consciousness, not consciousness society. As he put it, "It is not the consciousness of men that determines their being, but, on the contrary, their social being determines their consciousness." When the "Mode of Production" (the base) is transformed, the legal, political, religious and aesthetic beliefs of men (the superstructure) change also.

The Need for Revolution.
Marx saw class conflict between those owning the means of production (the bourgeoisie) and those selling the only thing they own, their labor (the proletariat) as the central fact of history. As he said in *The Communist Manifesto:*

> The history of all hitherto existing society is the history of class struggles. Freeman and slave, patrician and plebeian,

> lord and serf, guild-master and journeyman, in a word
> oppressor and oppressed, stood in constant opposition to
> one another, carried on an uninterrupted, now hidden, now
> open fight, a fight that each time ended either in a
> revolutionary reconstitution of society at large, or in the
> common ruin of the contending classes.

His solution was to have the working classes take control of
the state, gain control of the means of production, abolish all
classes (after a presumably short dictatorship of the proletariat)
and with it, abolish history. If history is defined as class
struggle and classes are eliminated, then history (as we have
known it) is abolished, so to speak. He also believed that the
state would wither away, eventually, when man had been
communized.

The Problem of Alienation.

The reason capitalism must be destroyed is because it produces
alienation in man. To quote Marx:

> . . . the division of labour offers us the first example of how, as
> long as man remains in natural society, that is, as long as a
> cleavage exists between the particular and the common interest,
> as long therefore as activity is not voluntary, but naturally,
> divided, man's own act becomes an alien power opposed to him,
> which enslaves him instead of being controlled by him.

There is a debate amongst Marxists as to whether the concept
of alienation is central to Marx's thought, or whether the need
for revolution is more important. Whatever the case, Marx's
ideas about alienation are critical, since alienation leads
individuals to have "false consciousness," and the system of
ideas and beliefs produced by this false consciousness

that Marx described as "ideology." In a capitalist society the
ideas of the ruling class are the ideas of the masses; the
bourgeoisie, by controlling the mode of production and system
of economic relations, control, in turn, the ideas of the
proletariat. Marx's attack on capitalism is based on ethics—his
belief that capitalism produced goods but along with it
alienation. As he says:

In what does this alienation of labour consist? First, that the work is *external* to the worker, that it is not part of his nature, that consequently he does not fulfill himself in his work but denies himself, has a feeling of misery, not of well being, does not develop freely a physical and mental energy but is physically exhausted and mentally debased.

So much for our brief explication of Marxism. What is important for us to recognize is that Marxists bring to the analysis of any social phenomenon an ideological position which enables them to interpret almost anything along certain lines. This kind of thinking is frequently described (in the case of Marxism or any ideology) as *doctrinaire*. What happens is that the ideology determines how a person will analyze a given problem. There is a prescribed method of analysis, just as there are prescribed answers, for all subjects. Once you accept the premises of the ideology (whether it be Marxism or One Hundred Percent Americanism or Capitalism), the rest follows almost automatically.

When you believe in an ideology, you know the answer, in a sense, before you are asked the question. It is this kind of straight jacketed thinking which disturbs non-ideological thinkers, though it might be argued that it is impossible to escape from some kind of an ideology. This is because analysis that is systematic and structured implies some kind of an ideology and thinking that is not systematic and coherent, that is "random," is frequently not worth very much.

It is this structure and coherence in ideologies that captivates people and accounts for the strong hold ideologies have on them. For the Marxist and for other ideologues, the world makes sense, history is moving in understandable ways, and the outcome of the historic confrontation between the capitalist and communist world is inevitable. It may even be that the *logic* or *structure* of the ideology is more important than the specific content, which explains why people can move, with such ease, from one ideological position to its polar opposite. Thus, Communists become right-wing conservatives (and vice versa) merely by doing a flip-flop and accepting the antithetical position. The content is different but the gratifications are the same, because the two systems are structurally similar.

An Application of Marxist Theory: Donald Duck

For an example of the way ideological thinking works, let us look at a book that came out a number of years ago: Dorfman and Mattelart's *How to Read Donald Duck: Imperialist Ideology in the Disney Comic.* This was written in Chile during the Allende period and deals with what the authors suggest is a hidden ideology in Donald Duck and other Disney works. The thesis of the book is that in the work of Disney the essentials of the bourgeois capitalist theory of politics and society are promulgated, though in a highly masked manner. That is, if you become a "duckologist" and read the adventures of Donald Duck in terms of their social and political significance, the values espoused, etc., you find that Disney is an apologist for capitalism.

For example, one of the basic ploys of bourgeois thinking is to suggest that phenomena which are historical are, instead, natural. What is natural cannot be changed, so being "natural" is a way of justifying laws and arrangements which benefit only small numbers of people, namely, the ruling class. The authors write "...ideas are conceived as products of a *natural* force. By making ideas appear beyond the control of the passive recipients and extrinsic to them, it takes the motors of history out of history into the realm of *pure nature.* This is called *inversion.* "

Generally the authors use some adventure in Donald Duck to back up their analysis. They treat the characters symbolically and the adventures as representative of general themes. Dorfman and Mattelart take up the theme of the consumption society as a means of explaining the appeal of Disney's characters:

> So the readers love these characters, which share all their own degradation and alienation, while remaining innocent little animals. Unable to control their own lives, or even the objects around them, the characters are perfectly closed around the nucleus of their imperfection. The egoism of the little animals, the defense of their individuality, their embroilment with private interests, provides a sense of distance between the characters and their creators, who are projecting their view of the world onto the animals. The reader as consumer of the lives of the animals

reproduces the sense of distance by feeling superior to and pity for the little animals.

An examination of *How to Read Donald Duck* reveals a basically Marxist structure and argument. That is, Marxist ideology is used to explain the significance of different characters and episodes and of Disney's work in general. Dorfman and Mattelart see Disney's social philosophy, that is, as basically destructive of the well-being of most of the people who read his comics because the messages in Disney are inherently propagandist.

He espouses a kind of individualism that is destructive of the good society, and so, ultimately, self-destructive. Donald Duck and his nephews and all the other characters are, unwittingly, secret agents of a bourgeois conspiracy to brainwash the masses in America as well as in the underdeveloped nations, which are importers of American culture and aspire to the "American Way of Life." Let me conclude this brief discussion of the book with a passage in which the ideological beliefs of the authors are made evident. This passage is little more than a rewriting of the formulations of Marx about the relationship between society and consciousness. As Dorfman and Mattelart put it:

> From the moment people find themselves involved in a certain social system—that is, from conception and birth—it is impossible for their consciousness to develop without being based on concrete material conditions. In a society where one class controls the means of economic production, that class also controls the means of intellectual production; ideas, feelings, intuitions, in short—the very meaning of life. The bourgeoisie have, in fact, tried to invert the true relationship between the material base and the superstructure. They conceive of ideas as productive of riches by means of the only untainted matter they know—grey matter—and the history of humanity becomes the history of ideas.

The conservative notion that that history is a record of ideas, violates Marx's belief that "society determines consciousness, not consciousness society."

How is one to "take" Dorfman and Mattelart? The book cites a number of reviews which see their analysis as absurd. This is to be expected since the idea of meaning in the comics—let alone political ideology—strikes many people as quite ridiculous. For Marxists, however, this study of Donald Duck makes eminently good sense, and is a pretty straight-forward ideological analysis of one aspect of what is often called "the culture industry" or "the consciousness industry."

There is really no resolution to the problem of ideology. Everyone has to have some theory of what makes society work. Even people who have not studied political theory generally have picked up, from their schooling, from the mass media and the whole culture establishment, a notion of what is important in the political arena and a political stance frequently associated with political parties and their platforms. The question we must ask is how coherent is the political thinking of the common man and woman and to what extent are their "ideologies" the product of a kind of conditioning or "brainwashing" of which they are unaware?

Rituals as Codes of Behavior
The term ritual is defined as an "established or prescribed procedure for a religious or other rite; a system of religious or other rites . . . [and] a prescribed code of behavior regulating social conduct. . . ." (*Random House Dictionary of the English Language, The Unabridged Edition*) The concept, which originally was used by anthropologists, has been adopted by many other kinds of social scientists who discuss political rituals, psychological compulsions and similarly structured behavior.

With ritual, as with the other concepts discussed here, the notion of a coherent, comprehensive, coded structure is what is paramount; it is this notion of a formal structure which unites ritual and role playing, identity and ideology. Though they are all different in terms of their content, their morphology (structure) has the same pattern of coherence and continuity— and all the other aspects of codes—that make it possible to describe them as kinds of codes.

It is difficult to be sure of the origin of many rituals, but their functions seem clear—rituals celebrate important events for persons (such as marriage) and for societies (such as services for soldiers who died in combat); they solidify groups; they tie people, emotionally, to groups and organizations; and they offer prescribed ways of behaving in given situations to alleviate anxiety and stress, amongst other things.

Rituals are particularly interesting because they are *sequences of actions* and so it is possible to examine them in terms of their structure, as well, say, as in terms of their consequences. Because rituals are embodiments of the beliefs of the people who practice them (either collectively or as individuals), they have a great deal to tell us, once we learn how to decipher them. Of course we must recognize that people do not always understand the full significance of the rituals in which they are participating, and sometimes do not even recognize that their behavior is ritualistic. That is, there are conscious rituals, as in religious and political celebrations, and there are unconscious rituals, as in the behavior of neurotics with various compulsions. All people have minor compulsions and "routines," but some people are literally slaves to their rituals and must follow elaborately structured patterns of behavior in order to avoid excessive anxiety.

For example, some people suffering from "repetition compulsion" follow elaborately prescribed rituals when doing simple things like bathing, which may take several hours. If disturbed in the middle of the ritual, or if he feels he hasn't performed it satisfactorily, the compulsive feels it necessary to repeat the ritual from the beginning. There are other situations in which the ritualistic nature of the activity has been internalized and the person acting ritually does not recognize how structured his behavior is, though he does not suffer from the torments of the compulsive person described above. Wherever we find a repeated, structured sequence of actions we can describe them as rituals, using the term in the broadest possible manner. Some people call these rituals "habits."

Many people develop a routine in washing up; the order in which you wash your face, brush your hair, brush your teeth— all of these generally are done in the same order year after year. A change in the order does not provoke uncontrollable nervous anxiety, though it may provoke irritation, and irritability.

In his classic study, *American Life: Dream and Reality,* W. Lloyd Warner analyzes our celebration of Memorial Day as a sacred ritual which helps unify a people characterized by a wide variety of different religions, each with its own sacred symbols and rituals and all, more or less in conflict with or in opposition to one another. Warner sees the Memorial Day celebrations as involving "the cult of the dead," and based on the theme of the "sacrifice" of the dead for the living.

Warner isolates a number of activities generally related to these celebrations: the sales of poppies, editorials citing dead soldiers from the diverse ethnic and socio-economic classes, "vacant chairs" at Lodge celebrations, sermons on sacrifice, etc.—culminating, finally, in the Memorial Day parade to a civic cemetery where people of all religions honor the dead. Warner provides a chart to show how different groups become progressively integrated, over time, during the period before Memorial Day. His thesis is:

> . . . that the Memorial Day ceremonies and subsidiary rites (such as those of Armistice Day) of today, yesterday, and tomorrow are rituals of a sacred symbol system which functions periodically to unify the whole community, with its conflicting symbols and its opposing, autonomous churches and associations. It is contended here that in the Memorial Day ceremonies the anxieties which man has about death are confronted with a system of sacred beliefs about death which gives the individuals involved and the collectivity of individuals a feeling of well-being.

Thus, if Warner is correct, Memorial Day is a national sacred ritual which enables diverse groups to integrate themselves into the greater American community, and which provides feelings of well being for the groups and the individual members of the groups as well.

The people involved in the Memorial Day celebrations do not necessarily recognize the ritualistic nature of all the celebrations, but they do feel the power generated by them—in this case, a strong identification with American society and its historical experience. Rituals, then, are chains of actions or sequences of actions which can be examined in terms of their structure as well as their functions. They are coded behavior, and understanding the code helps us to understand the meaning of the ritual. The same kind of structural analysis can be applied to myths, folktales and various popular art forms—all of which have a variety of elements in combination. In fact, there are an immense number of activities which form what is called "everyday life" that are accessible to this technique. But before I turn to this material in the next section of this study, I would like to briefly sum up the argument of this chapter— namely, that there is a core uniting the concepts from the different disciplines which have been discussed.

Culture codes as a Unifying Factor in the Social Sciences

In this brief section I would like to suggest that *culture codes*, the secret structures which I described earlier, are a unifying factor in the social sciences. It is a commonplace that the various disciplines in the social sciences are arbitrary and are matters more of convenience than anything else; thus, the traditional perspectives in the social sciences, which divide humanity up into a number of *aspects*, have a historic rather than a logical reason for being.

If, instead of looking at the content of the disciplines, we examine their structure, we find that they all have (at least in terms of the topics discussed here) what we have called *codes* in common. That is, we have been able to define each of our topics—identity, social roles, etc., as a kind of code. The characteristics of culture codes, once again, are: *coherence, covertness, clarity, continuity, comprehensiveness* and *communicability*. All of these were discussed in some detail in the first chapter.

The descriptions of each concept as a kind of code follows:

> *Personal Identity* is a private code
>
> *Social Roles* are Identity Codes;
>
> *Institutions* are Regulatory Codes in Structured Relationships;
>
> *Ideologies* are Socio-Political Codes; and
>
> *Rituals* are Codes of Behavior Regulating Social Conduct.

Like all attempts to organize material, this unification has an element of artificiality about it and is a simplification. But it does suggest a number of concepts from a number of different disciplines within the social sciences do have something in common. It is a step towards a greater, more profound integration.

The principle thesis of the sociology of knowledge is that there are modes of thought which cannot be adequately understood as long as their social origins are obscured. It is indeed true that only the individual is capable of thinking. There is no such metaphysical entity as a group mind which thinks over and above the heads of individuals, or whose ideas the individual merely reproduces. Nevertheless, it would be false to deduce from this that all the ideas and sentiments which motivate an individual have their origin in him alone, and can be adequately explained solely on the basis of his own life-experience....

Only in a quite limited sense does the single individual create out of himself the mode of speech and of thought we attribute to him. He speaks the language of his group; he thinks in the manner in which his group thinks. He finds at his disposal only certain words and their meanings. These not only determine to a large extent the avenues of approach to the surrounding world, but they also show at the same time from which angle and in which context of activity objects have hitherto been perceptible and accessible to the group or the individual....

Strictly speaking it is incorrect to say that the single individual thinks. Rather it is more correct to insist that he participates in thinking further what other men have thought before him. He finds himself in an inherited situation with patterns of thought which are appropriate to this situation and attempts to elaborate further the inherited modes of response or to substitute others for them in order to deal more adequately with the new challenges which have arisen out of shifts and changes in his situation. Every individual is therefore in a two-fold sense predetermined by the fact of growing up in a society: on the one hand he finds a ready-made situation and on the other he finds in that situation preformed patterns of thought and conduct. (pp.2, 3)

Karl Mannheim, *Ideology and Utopia*

Chapter 4:

How Did You Become Yourself?

Pop Culture and the Psyche

In this chapter I will deal with the following topics:

> How people obtain their identities
> Repetition Compulsion and our immersion in popular culture
> The various meanings of the term "popular"
> The various meanings of the term "culture"
> Travel literature as a means of capturing cultural differences

I will start with that most fascinating of questions—how do we become ourselves? How do we arrive at the persons we are, at any moment in time? How do we achieve an identity?

How do we become ourselves?
It's an interesting question. How did you become yourself? Many people would answer this by saying something like "I don't know."

Someone from France once asked me, "What was your formation?" That term, "formation," suggests that people don't create themselves as much as may think they do. What happens, instead, is that they are "formed" somehow by their culture, by the society in which they grow up, by the circumstances of their birth (including their birth order), their gender, their family, their religion, the town or city where they were born and the state (in America) or the country and region of the country in which they were raised, the language they learned and countless other variables. If we all find ourselves, as Mannheim suggested in *Ideology and Utopia,* predetermined by a "ready made situation" and "preformed patterns of thought and conduct," how do we achieve some kind of a distinctive identity?

As a wit once said, "the idea of the self-made man (and woman) relieves God of a lot of responsibility." And it does!

There is also the matter of our inborn (physical, genetic, whatever you wish to call them) natures--the attributes of our selves that are "hard wired," so to speak, in people. I have two children and they are as different as night and day. How does one explain this? Well, for one thing, one is a female (the firstborn) and the other is a male. So there is birth order and gender to consider. But they each have radically different personalities and interests, and these differences stem to a considerable degree, I would say, from their basic natures. It may all stem from their genes? There was something in each of them, I would suggest, that stems from their different intrinsic selves and cannot be explained by gender, birth order, where they grew up and so on. My point, then, is that we have to give nature her due in the so-called "nature-nurture" debate. But only to a point. Nurture plays a big role, too.

I once asked a young boy "How did you turn out the way you did?" He looked at me with a puzzled expression on his face. Then he said, "I was just lucky, I guess." And that probably is the way most of us feel about ourselves. "We were just lucky!" But maybe, in some respects, we weren't? We might not be lucky as far as the family we're born into or in terms of our genetic makeup or in any number of other respects--what we look like, what our personalities are, where we live, and so on.

Repetition Compulsion
Sigmund Freud used the term "repetition compulsion" to explain the behavior of certain kinds of people who cannot

help repeating earlier experiences, most of which generally are painful. This concept is described in the *Encyclopedia of Psychoanalysis* (Ludwig Eidelberg, MD, Editor- in- Chief) as follows:(Free Press, 1968:374, 375):

> Repetition Compulsion refers to an active repetition of a passively experienced unpleasure. Fine (1962) pointed out that this active repetition "helps the individual master the anxiety involved in passively suffering some trauma" (narcissistic mortification). In some cases, cited by Freud, an aggressive pleasure was achieved; in others, at least unpleasure was eliminated....Freud (1926) regarded the repetition compulsion as operating to promote the dominating function of the mental apparatus, i.e., to bind tension and eliminate excitation. He viewed it as an expression of the Nirvana Principle, and as a derivative of the ultimate aim of the aggressive (death) instincts, the return to an inorganic state. Clinical manifestations of the repetition compulsion may be seen in children's play, traumatic neuroses, the transference neurosis, and neuroses in general (especially the fate neuroses). Children's play is frequently devoted to the active repetition of passively experienced traumatic events: for example, the game of doctor is played by a child who has just received an injection...

I mention this matter of repetition compulsion for two reasons. First, on the personal level, I wonder whether my career of writing about popular culture and the media for more than 45 years has an element of repetition compulsion in it. Is there something in my psyche that makes me write about these topics (as well as humor and lately tourism) over and over again, in different books and with different emphases, but still on the same topic. I keep on writing about popular culture because I keep finding new things to write about and new ways to write about it. In part, because popular culture is such a large, amorphous, hard to define and pin down, hard to come to grips with and explain, subject. And in part because new genres are created, new fads take over and there are always lots of new matters to be investigated.

Someone once suggested that all writers write the same book, over and over again, but in different ways. So my fascination with the subject of popular culture and the media and my inability to escape from it, may be due to the fact that I'm a writer and all my books are, in some vague way, variation of some basic or UR Berger book.   I became interested in popular culture, sometimes described as mass-mediated culture, because I had the sense that it plays a major role in socializing people, that it--more than many other things--is what helps us become what we are. I saw an article in a Sunday supplement that was argued "Parents Come in Third: Genes and Peers are Basic." One question that comes to mind, of course, is how did peers become the persons they became? How did those peers, who allegedly influence us so much, arrive at themselves?

If I were to ask you, "how did you become yourself?" after you said "I was lucky, I guess," I'd probe deeper and probably find that popular culture and the mass media played a major role in shaping your psyche and character. The   second aspect of   "repetition compulsion" that interests me involves the enormous amount of media we consume on a daily basis. Is there some element of "repetition compulsion" behind all the radio we listen to, the television we watch, the music we hear or play for ourselves on our stereo systems, the comics and newspapers and magazines we read, and so on.

The average American is involved with media around eight hours a day. So, I ask--are we using the media--without recognizing what we are doing, of course--to help us deal with some traumas we experienced and have forgotten about, some problems we face, or some unconscious anxieties and desires we have? Repetition compulsion involves, let us remember, the unconscious. We are seldom aware of the roots of our behavior. And while we may recognize, at times, some kind of a habitual (or even compulsive nature) to our behavior, we are not, as a rule, aware that the cause of much of our behavior—if the psychoanalysts are correct--is buried deep in our psyches.

The Meanings of the Term "Popular"

The term "popular" is a rather complicated one; almost as complicated as the term "culture," which I'll discuss shortly. "Popular" comes from the Latin term *popularis,* which means "people." There are several meanings connected with the term popular: first, involving the people in general; second, suitable for the people (in that sense that it is easy to comprehend); third, having widespread acceptance or appeal.

A thesaurus offers a number of other aspects of the term such as: "approved," " beloved," "common," "customary," "desired," "famous," "fashionable," "lay," "prevalent," "public," and "usual." And for the related term "popularize," it suggests "explain," "vulgarize," and "make understandable." We see, then, that *popular* contains a number of different meanings.

When critics write about popular culture, they tend to use it in a negative sense—works of art that are easy to understand, that cater to the "lowest common denominator," that are vulgar, trite, formulaic, sexist, superficial and so on. A number of years ago I wrote an article that was titled "Why is Popular Culture So Unpopular?" My point was that popular culture is "unpopular" with elites who tend to look down upon the public and particularly upon public taste in art, literature, film, theater, and so on. Popular culture is, of course, very popular with the general public (or "populace") for whom it is created.

What's important to understand is that criticism of popular culture on the taste level will almost always find it inferior to "elite" works of art; that's a given, most of the time. Popular culture is worth studying because of its role in shaping people's identities, in giving people ideas about what's good and bad, what's beautiful and ugly, what's important and trivial, and so on. That is, we study popular culture because of its role in socializing and enculturating people, because of what it reflects about culture and society (or about subcultures and other groups of people). Popular culture also has played a role in shaping so-called "elite" culture so there are even aesthetic reasons for investigating popular culture. And, of course, some popular culture is aesthetically satisfying, too. It isn't all junk—though most of it is!

In the chart below, I suggest (in a somewhat oversimplified way) the differences between popular culture—that is, popular works of art or mass-mediated works of art-- and elite works of art as elite critics see things. To make things simple, we can think of two works: Shakespeare's *Hamlet* and the film *Avatar*   I am taking two extreme examples to make my point and to clarify things. But we could do the same even with less extreme examples.

Popular Works of Art	Elite Works of Art
Avatar	*Hamlet*
Mass produced	Works of individual artists & creators
Mass mediated	Not mass mediated as a rule
Lowest Common Denominator	For refined sensibilities
Short life in media	Timeless
Little insight into human nature	Brilliant insights into human nature
Simple minded	Incredibly complex

Works of Popular Culture & Elite Culture Contrasted

I realize, of course, that I have taken extreme *texts* (the term academic critics use for plays, movies, poems, comic books, advertisements, videos, and so on) to make my point. If we make a film of *Hamlet* and it is shown is movie houses, then later on television, we have what was originally an elite text shown in a mass medium. Does that mean it is now popular culture? In the last few decades, our attitudes about films have changed. When they were "movies" they were seen as popular culture; when they became "film" (as in "art films") they were seen as works of elite culture. The point is, a given medium can be used for both popular and elite culture. It's not the medium that's crucial—it's the text! If I had chosen Orson Welles' film, *Citizen Kane,* or Alfred Hitchcock's *Vertigo* (which has recently replaced *Citizen Kane* as "the best film ever made") the polarity sketched out above would not be correct. Since I have used the term "culture" a good deal, it is worth considering the various meanings of "culture." After all, popular culture is a kind of culture!

Culture
Culture is one of the more complicated words we will be dealing with. One of the problems we encounter is that there are a number of different meanings attached to the term. We think of culture two ways: one in terms of aesthetic matters (relative to the arts) and also as a concept used by anthropologists to describe a people's way of life. There are something like a hundred different definitions of culture used by anthropologists, so I understand.

The word "culture" comes from the Latin *cultus,* which means "care" and from the French *colere* which means "to till" as in "till the ground." There are a number of words associated with culture. For example, there is the term "cult" which suggests something religious or sacred. We are continually amazed at the power cults have to shape people's behavior, to brainwash them—to turn intelligent and educated people into fanatics. Here we are dealing with the power of charismatic personalities and of groups over individuals. If cults can exercise enormous power over individuals and groups of people, can't we say that cultures also can do the same thing, though not to as extreme a degree, generally speaking.

There is also the term "cultivated," which means either growing something or, in the realm of aesthetics and the arts, sophisticated taste. Just as many plants only exist because they are cared for by some cultivator, over a period of time, so people's taste and cultivation only are developed by education and training. It takes time to develop a refined sensibility, to become discriminating, to appreciate texts that are difficult and complex and not immediately satisfying.

Bacteriologists also speak about cultures, but they use the term to describe the bacteria that are grown in Petri dishes if they are given suitable media (sources of nourishment). This matter of bacteria growing in media may be an important metaphor for us: just as bacteria need media to grow into culture, so do human beings need cultures to survive and develop themselves. We don't do it all on our own—even though there is much talk of individualism (a concept we learn from our cultures) and the so-called self-made man and woman.

In the chart below I show the interesting parallels:

Bacteriology	Sociology/Anthropology
Bacteria	Humans
Grow in media	Affected by media
Form cultures	Form cultures

Of course we are much more complex than bacteria; in truth, each of us form a kind of medium for countless kinds of bacteria and other micro-organisms that inhabit our mouths and various other parts of our bodies. Bacteriology involves the cultivation and study of micro-organisms (bacteria) in prepared nutrients and the study of media (what is often called cultural criticism nowadays) involves the study of individuals and groups in a predominantly, but not completely, mass-mediated culture. Not all culture is mass mediated.

Let me offer a typical anthropological definition of culture. This one is quite old but it is useful because it covers most of the bases. It is by Henry Pratt Fairchild and appeared in his *Dictionary of Sociology and Related Sciences* (1967:80):

> A collective name for all behavior patterns socially acquired and transmitted by means of symbols; hence a name for all the distinctive achievements of human groups, including not only such items as language, tool-making, industry, art, science, law, government, morals and religion, but also the material instruments or artifacts in which cultural achievements are embodied and by which intellectual cultural features are given practical effect, such as buildings, tools, machines, communication devices, art objects, etc.

Let's consider some of the topics Fairchild mentions.

> ***Behavior Patterns.***   We are talking about codes and patterns of behavior here that are found in groups of people.

> ***Socially Acquired.***   We are taught these behavior patterns as we grow up in a family in some geographical location and are profoundly affected by the family we are born into, its religion, and all kinds of other matters.

> ***Transmitted by Means of Symbols.***   This refers to language and works of art, both of which have a profound impact on our psyches and our consciousness. It also can be understood to refer to communication of all kinds and involving all media: spoken words, facial expression, mass mediated, and so on.

The Distinctive Achievements of Human Groups. This is important because it points out that it is in groups that we become human and become enculturated or acculturated (two words for the same thing, for all practical purposes). We have our own distinctive natures but we are also part of society.

Artifacts in which cultural achievements are embodied. The artifacts we are talking about here are the popular culture texts carried in the various media and other non-mediated aspects of popular culture (or not directly mediated) such as fashions in clothes, food, art, objects (what anthropologists call "material culture") language use, sexual practices and related matters. We know that a lot of our popular culture, while not carried by the media, is nevertheless profoundly affected by it.

We can see, then, that popular culture is a very complicated matter that plays some kind of a role in shaping our consciousness and our behavior. When I say "our" behavior, I mean my behavior and your behavior. You may think you are immune from the impact of the media and popular culture, but that is a delusion that is generated, I would suggest, by the media. The great English poet W.H. Auden once wrote these chilling lines:

> "Each in the prison of himself is convinced of his own freedom."

We think we are not affected by the media and popular culture (sometimes called mass mediated culture) but we are wrong. We must make a distinction between affected by and determined by here. Popular culture affects us but it doesn't necessarily determine every act we do…though some scholars, who believe the media are very powerful, might argue with this point.

Falling Off The Map

For a graphic example of how cultures differ, let me offer two quotations from the Indian travel writer Pico Iyer. They come from his book *Falling Off the Map: Some Lonely Places of the World,* a collection of travel articles about seldom-visited places (by American travelers, at least) he wrote for various publications. I'll start with his description of Saigon.

> *Saigon*
> ...the only word for Saigon is "wild." One evening I counted more than a hundred two-wheel vehicles racing past me in the space of sixty seconds, speeding around the jam-packed streets as if on some crazy merry-go-round, a mad carnival without a ringmaster; I walked into a dance club and found myself in the midst of a crowded floor of hip gay boys in sleeveless T-shirts doing the latest moves to David Byrne; outside again, I was back inside the generic Asian swirl, walking through tunnels of whispers and hisses. "You want boom-boom?" "Souvenir for you dah-ling?" "Why you not take special massage?" Shortly before midnight, the taxi girls stream out of their nightclubs in their party dresses and park their scooters outside the hotels along "Simultaneous Uprising" Street. Inside, Indian and Malaysian and Japanese fair-trade delegates huddle in clusters, circling like excited schoolboys and checking out the mini-skirted wares, while out on the street legless beggars hop about, and cripple girls offer oral services and boys of every stripe mutter bargains for their sisters. One wanders, dazed, as through some Fellini night-world, beautiful women in golden ao dais waving slowly from slow moving *cyclos.*

Compare this description of Saigon with his portrait of Reykjavik, Iceland, equally as fascinating and fantastic but considerably different from Saigon.

> *Reykjavik, Iceland*
> Even "civilization" seems to offer no purchase for the mind here: nothing quite makes sense. Iceland boasts the largest number of poets, presses, and readers per capita in the world: Reykjavik, a town smaller than Rancho Cucamonga, California, has five daily newspapers, and to the match the literary production of Iceland, the U.S. would have to publish twelve hundred new books *a day.* Iceland has the

oldest living language in Europe—its people read the medieval sagas as if they were tomorrow's newspaper—and all new concepts, such as "radio" and "telephone," are given poetical medieval equivalents.   Roughly three eldest children in every four are illegitimate here, and because every son of Kristjan is called Kristjansson, and every daughter Kristjansdottir, mothers always have different surnames from their children (and in any case are rarely living with the fathers)...The first day I ever spent in "Surprise City" (as Reykjavik is called), I found golden-haired princesses and sword-wielding knights enacting fairy-tale sagas on the main bridge in the capital; I cam within two feet of the president (who seems, unguarded in the street, just another elegant blond single mother)...The Salvation Army hostel is only four doors away from the Parliament building here, and the Parliament building itself is a modest two-story house with a doorman less imposing than those in the nearby pubs.

We can see that there are considerable differences between Saigon and Reykjavik, just as (to be fair) Iyer points out the incredible differences between cities in Vietnam, such as the differences between Saigon and Hue. Iyer's description of the landscape of Iceland may help explain the national character of the Icelanders. As he writes: (1993:67):

> I knew, before I visited, a little about the epidemic oddness of the place: there was no beer In Iceland in 1987, and no television on Thursdays; there were almost no trees, and no vegetables. Iceland is an ungodly wasteland of volcanoes and tundra and Geysir, the mother of geysirs, a country so lunar that NASA astronauts did their training there.

There has to be some influence of this remarkable landscape and climate, of the Iceland geographical location, the amount of light and darkness in which people live, upon the people who live there. In the same light, there has to be some influence of the jungle and the climate of Vietnam on its people.

What we become is, it seems to me, due to some curious combination of factors involving our natures (that is, the hard-wired elements of our personalities) and our cultures, with the matter of chance playing a big role as well. Think, for example, how different our lives would be if we had AIDS or were born with a severe "deformity." A baby born in Saigon but raised in Reykjavik would be considerably different when he or she grew up than a baby born in Reykjavik but raised in Saigon—in everything from preferences for foods, attitudes towards sex, languages spoken and understood, and so on. Where we are located on some map, it turns out, plays an important role in our lives.

So culture makes a difference. And popular culture is the aspect of culture or kind of culture or manifestation of culture that seems to have the most immediate impact upon us. Consider, for example, the amount of popular culture we are exposed to and involved with in our daily lives. I will offer a hypothetical example—the story of an average American's typical day.

An Average American's Typical Day of Media Usage
Let's take an example of a typical day in a typical American male—John Q. Public. In this case, a fictional American who is representative of most Americans. In the morning, he is awakened by a clock radio and he listens to the radio (if he doesn't watch morning shows on television) while he gets dressed. And then he has breakfast. He may also read the morning newspaper for a while. While he drives to work, he probably listens to the radio, also. This "drive-time" period probably lasts around 30 or 45 minutes, each way. Thus, it is reasonable to assume somewhere between an hour and a half and two hours of radio listening in an average day.

If he is an average television viewer, he watches around four hours a day. This means, if he gets home at 6:00 PM and goes to bed at 11:00 PM, four of those five hours are devoted to watching television. He may, of course, watch television in the morning, just after he gets up. That may take up part of his four hours. In addition, during a typical day, Johnny reads a newspaper for a while, looks at some magazines, may read for a while and also listen to some music. It is possible that he reads a magazine while he listens to music on his stereo (or the radio) or "watches" television. What follows is a statistical table showing the typical media usage of Americans, based on statistics obtained on the Internet. .

Below I offer a chart on media usage by eight to eighteen year olds that is based on research by the Kaiser Foundation.

TOPIC	2009	2004	1999
TV content	4:29	3:05	3:47
Music/Audio	3:31	1:44	1:48
Computer	1:29	1:02	:27
Video Games	1:13	:49	:26
Print	:38	:43	:43
Movies	:25	:25	:25
TOTAL MEDIA EXPOSURE	**10:45**	**8:33**	**7:29**
MULTITASKING PROPORTION	29%	26%	16%
TOTAL MEDIA USE	**7:38**	**6:21**	**6:13**

8- 18 Year Olds Average Amount of Media Use Per Day

The figure of 10:45 hours for each day reflects an increase of around two hours of media exposure per day in 2009 over 2004. Because young people multi-task, the total amount of media usage ends up at 7.38 hours per day—almost the equivalent of a full day's work.

This comes to almost eight hours of exposure to media and popular culture in a typical day. Obviously, this is an enormous amount of time in which we are involved with, immersed in, exposed to—whatever you wish to call it-- popular culture, especially in its mass mediated form. Is it possible that our exposure to all this popular culture and mass media has no effect upon us?

The question now arises—how does this popular culture affect us? It is that question I will consider in the next chapter.

Those persons who talk most about human freedom are those who are actually most blindly subject to social determination, inasmuch as they do not in most cases suspect the profound degree to which their conduct is determined by their interests. In contrast to this it should be noted that it is precisely those who insist on the unconscious influence of the social determinants of conduct, who strive to overcome these determinants as much as possible. They uncover unconscious motivations in order to make those forces which formerly rules them more and more into objects of conscious rational decision. (p. 48)

Karl Mannheim, *Ideology and Utopia*

Chapter 5:

Popular Culture and Personality

The topics covered in this chapter all involve the various ways popular culture affects our minds, our psyches, and our personalities. I will discuss:

> Metaphor and the role of analogies in our thinking
> The power of identification with symbolic heroes and heroines (and celebrities)
> Mimesis—the power of imitation
> Mimetic Desire: our imitation of the *desire* of others
> Models we imitate consciously and unconsciously
> The power of images
> The power of information
> The power of stories (narratives)
> The power of spectacles
> How concepts work and affect us
> The power of music

Is it possible that we can be immersed in popular culture to the extent that we are without being affected, in rather profound ways, by it? There are some critics who argue that our exposure to media and popular culture is not terribly important. Yes, we watch many hours of television every day and yes, we listen to the radio a lot, and yes, we listen to music on our stereos, and yes, we go to lots of movies and maybe we read lots of comic books, murder mysteries, science fiction and other popular fiction, and yes, we spend an hour or so each day using our cell phones to text others and consumer media, but no, the impact of all this is, in the end, trivial.

On the Power of Metaphor: It's All in the Game.
Metaphors are figures of speech that involve comparisons between two things. We find metaphors in poetry, where poets write "my life is a red rose." In metaphor the comparison is very strong: there is an equal sign between two things:

> my love = a red rose.

There is a weaker form of metaphor, called simile, in which a comparison is made using *like* or *as*. Here we find phrases such as:

> my love is *like* a red rose
> my love is *as* a red rose

What we have to realize is that these comparisons are important, not trivial matters. I say that because there is good reason to argue that metaphor has a major role in shaping our thinking and our behavior. Thus, in *Metaphors We Live By,* George Lakoff and Mark Johnson (1980:3) write:

> Most people think they can get along perfectly well without metaphor. We have found, on the contrary, that metaphors are pervasive in everyday life, not just in language but thought and action. Our ordinary conceptual system, in terms of which we both think and act, is fundamentally metaphoric in nature. The concepts that govern our thought are not just matters of the intellect. They also govern our everyday functioning down to the most mundane details. Our concepts structure what we perceive, how we get around in the world, and how we relate to other people. Our conceptual system thus plays a central role in defining our everyday realities.

This passage points out the important role metaphoric thinking plays in our lives—even though we may not recognize that our thinking is metaphoric or that there is a link between metaphor, our thinking and our behavior.

But our behavior is connected to the ideas we have about how we should behave and what we've learned from our culture about how we should behave. Thus, let me offer an example. Let's take a song that I used to listen to, over and over again, when I was growing up: "It's All in the Game" which has lyrics to the effect that love is a game. If love is a game, it means that love involves various aspects of playing games. And what are some of the characteristics of games? Let me suggest some of them:

People cheat in games. Not everyone plays fair in games and likewise, if love is a game, we shouldn't expect people involved in a love affair not to cheat. We know that people often do "cheat" on their lovers—but is this behavior to expected or condoned? It seems that half the country western songs one hears are about lovers who cheat on one another or who have "cheating hearts."

Games end after a while. Games don't last forever, and thus love should be seen as something that one plays for a while, but terminates when one is bored with the game or for some other reason. If we see love as a game that is destined to end, it colors our notion of how to relate to our lovers. Does this mean we "use" lovers and then dump them when we're tired of the game?

There are winners and losers in games. What does it mean to "lose" in love? Or "win" in love? This notion, that there are winners and losers, suggests that love is, somehow, a battle between rivals, each intent on winning. That is, love involves fighting for dominance and one party will be dominant and the other party will end up as submissive.

Games have rules. In order to play a game, there have to be mutually accepted rules that govern the game. But who determines what the rules of "love" are and how one interprets them? We learn about love from our exposure to popular culture, among other things. All we hear, hour after hour, on the radio are songs about love and these songs contain ideas and metaphors that give us our ideas about the nature of love.

Games often take place in certain locations. We play games (such as Monopoly) on boards that shape the games. And we play games on courts (basketball), in stadiums (baseball, football) and other special sites. Thus, there is some question about where we play the "game" of love? In restaurants? In bedrooms? And do we make a distinction between "love" and "sex" and if so, what is the difference?

Games involve strategy and deception. If love is a game, then logic tells us it is acceptable to use deception and various strategies to "win" the game—however we may define winning.

These points all suggest that the metaphor "love is a game" has logical implications that may have a profound influence on the way people think about love and the way they act when they are involved in love affairs. We have a code here that involves the logical implications of premises. What makes the power of metaphor so pernicious is that people do not recognize that they are being shaped, somehow, by the metaphors they hear and often adopt as models for their behavior. That is, people who listen to a song such as "All in the Game" do not recognize that their ideas have been affected, in any way, by the song. In the same way, we do not realize the degree to which our consciousness has been affected by metaphors and other ideas found in songs and other forms of popular culture.

On the power of identification with symbolic heroes, heroines and celebrities

When we are young, it is quite natural to identify with symbolic heroes and heroines (and perhaps also celebrities) with whom we come in contact in popular culture. These heroes and heroines, many of whom are fictional (found in stories we are read as children, comic books, television shows, films, etc.) are strong, good looking, and generally achieve great things and gain great admiration. The heroines are usually beautiful and talented.

The term "identification" is generally defined as a process in which someone becomes like someone else. As Charles Brenner explains in *An Elementary Textbook of*

Psychoanalysis (Revised Edition, 1973: 41), "By "identification" we mean the act or process of becoming like something or someone in one or several aspects of thought or behavior." When we identify with powerful heroic figures, we "participate," so to speak, in the power and glory of these heroic figures. Thus, we derive a kind of "halo" effect from identifying with a character like Superman or Spider Man or Wonder woman. A weak and relatively powerless child escapes from this status by identifying with Superman or some other hero or heroine. Some of these heroes and heroines may be sports figures—wonderful baseball players, football players, basketball players, tennis players, and so on.

I discovered, when giving a lecture tour of the Scandinavian countries a number of years ago, that the young son of one of the professors I was visiting knew all the important pro basketball players. As we develop, and go through various stages in our lives, these heroic figures with whom we identify, may change considerably—depending upon our stage of development at the time. This process of identification is something we are not aware of, even though it is very important to us. Ultimately, it helps us liberate ourselves from the domination of our parents, and, Jungians would argue, in particular our mothers. But young children don't know what the concept "identification" means. They do, however, know how to identify with heroes and heroines. The code is: find a hero to identify with.

As Joseph Henderson explains in "Ancient Myths and Modern Man" (in Carl G. Jung, *Man and His Symbols, 1968, Dell Books,* page 111):

> In the developing consciousness of the individual the hero figure is the symbolic means by which the emerging ego overcomes the inertia of the conscious mind, and liberates the mature man from a progressive longing to return to the blissful state of infancy in a world dominated by his mother.

What Henderson points out is that heroes and heroines of all kinds help us separate ourselves from our mothers and parents and enable us to become individuals and grow up. What this process of identification with heroic figures (male and female as well as animals, etc.) from popular culture is of considerable importance to us and not, by any means, a trivial matter. At a very early age, now, many young children in America spend hours watching television programs with heroic figures; in addition, we read stories to our children, and they learn about other heroic figures in nursery school and kindergarten.

Thus, it is reasonable to suggest that popular culture plays an important role in socializing Americans from a very early age. Unfortunately, not all the socialization done by popular culture is good for children; in fact, one might argue just the opposite. For the most part, what children learn from television, video games, films and other popular culture and media tends to be quite destructive of their well being.

Mimesis or Imitation

Mimesis is the Latin term for "imitation" which is one of the more important theories of art. In his *Poetics*, Aristotle suggests that the arts are based on imitation. He writes: (quoted in Smith and Parks, *The Great Critics,* 3rd Edition, 1951) "Epic poetry and Tragedy, Comedy also and Dithyrambic poetry, and the music of the flute and of the lyre in most of their forms are all in their general conception modes of imitation." (p.28) If art is an imitation of life, this gives it, M.H. Abrams suggests, a lower status than life itself.

Abrams has written an influential book, *The Mirror and the Lamp: Romantic_Theory and the Critical Tradition,* which offers four fundamental critical orientations, including mimesis. These are:

1. **Mimetic Theories of Art**. In Abrams' typology, those who believe in "mimetic" theories of art suggest it is a "mirror."

2. **Objective Theories of Art**. These theorists argue that rather than imitating reality like a mirror, art projects its own more-or-less self-contained reality. It is thus opposed to the mirror and is represented by the "lamp." As Abrams writes: (1958:26)

> ...the "objective orientation," which on principle regards the work of art in isolation from all...external points of

> reference, analyzes it as a self-sufficient entity constituted by its parts in their internal relations, and sets out to judge it solely by criteria intrinsic to its own mode of being.

We are close to the notion that art exists only for art's sake.

3. **Pragmatic Theories of Art.** These theories suggest that art is functional, that it does things, such as teaching us about life, instilling moral values in people, persuading us to do certain things and so on. As Abrams explains things: (1958, 20, 21)

> The pragmatic orientation, ordering the aim of the artist and the character of the work to the nature, the needs, and the springs of pleasure in the audience, characterized by far the greatest part of criticism from the time of Horace from the time of Horace through the eighteenth century.

4. **Expressive Theories of Art.** These theories focus on the creators of works of art and the creative processes, along with the emotional kicks that works of art generate in people. Thus Abrams points out that: (1958:21,22)

> Almost all the major critics of the English romantic generation phased definitions or key statements showing a parallel alignment from work to poet. Poetry is the overflow, utterance, or projection of the thought and feelings of the poet; or else (in the chief variant formulation) poetry is defined in terms of the imaginative process, which modifies and synthesizes the images, thoughts and feelings of the poet.

There are, then, two sets of opposing theories of art here: first, the mimetic and the objective and, secondly, the pragmatic and the emotive. The word "POEM" is a handy mnemonic device for remembering these theories, though the word "MOPE" places them in their relationships more accurately.

Although Abrams writes about literature and theories that focused on literature, we can extend the range and use these four theories to analyze the mass media and interpret the texts carried by the media.   We can also see that many of the theories of art developed in recent years can be traced back to these four basic theories. For example, it can be suggested that auteur theory, which focuses on the role of the director in film-making, is essentially an expressive theory of art.

Abrams also offers a diagram that, he suggests, shows how these theories relate to one another in an over-arching framework.

UNIVERSE

WORK

ARTIST   AUDIENCE

Note: there should be lines between universe and work and work and artists and audience.

If we line these elements up against his four theories we arrive at the following set of relationships:

Theory of Art	Focus in Work of Art
Mimetic	Universe
Objective	Work
Pragmatic	Audience
Expressive	Artist

Since Abrams was dealing with literature and printed texts, he did not include media in his formulations. If media is added, we move from a triangle to a rectangle, with media in the center, relating to and tied to all four corners of the rectangle.

I would suggest we also modify the term universe and make it society, so we can focus on the relationship that exists between a text, its audience and society, at large. A revision I have made of Abrams's diagram is shown below:

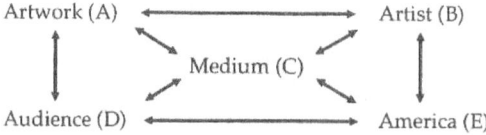

This chart enables us to discuss texts in terms of their creators, the media that carry them, their audiences and society at large.

I have used alliteration here as a mnemonic device. Every element can be connected, either directly or indirectly, with every other element in this chart.

Mimetic Desire

With mimetic desire, we take the notion of imitation a step further. We are familiar with the notion that mimesis involves imitation from the words "mime" and "mimic." Mimes are performers who imitate certain activities without saying anything to explain what they are doing. And mimics imitate—so as to ridicule, generally--someone's speech, body language, According to the French critic René Girard, who developed the concept and explained its importance in his book *A Theater of Envy* (Oxford University Press, 1991: page 3)

> When we think of those phenomena in which mimicry is likely to play a role, we enumerate such things as dress, mannerisms, facial expressions, speech, stage acting, artistic creation, and so forth, but we never think of desire. Consequently, we see imitation in social life as a force for gregariousness and bland conformity through the mass reproduction of a few social models.

> If imitation plays a role in desire, if it contaminates our urge to acquire and possess, this conventional view, while not entirely false, misses the main point. Imitation does not merely draw people together, it pulls them apart. Paradoxically, it can do these two things simultaneously. Individuals who desire the same thing are united by something so powerful that, as long as they can share whatever they desire, they remain the best of friends; as soon as they cannot, they become the worst of enemies.

Girard's book is about Shakespeare's plays. Girard argues that the basic force motivating the characters in Shakespeare is mimetic desire; it is the key to understanding Shakespeare, and *A Theater of Envy* examines Shakespeare's plays and shows how mimetic desire informs and pervades them.

Remember, mimetic desire means that people desire objects not for their intrinsic or essential value but, in essence, because someone else desires them; we imitate the desire of others in mimetic desire. Thus, as Girard explains, in the story of Helen of Troy: (1991:123)

> The only reasons the Greeks want her back is because the Trojans want to keep her. The only reason the Trojans want to keep her is because the Greeks want her back. All mimetic circles are vicious circles....

We have to make a distinction between mimetic desire and envy. Envy is always mimetic but not all mimetic desire is based on envy. That is because, as Girard sees things, mimetic desire is so complex and assumes so many different forms that to say it is the same thing as envy is too reductionistic.

It is possible, Girard suggests, for us to see mimetic desire as functioning in advertising. Audiences of television commercials and print advertisements are premised upon our desiring what those we see in advertising desire—that is, upon our identifying with and imitating the desire of the actors and actresses in advertising. That is, the underlying reason behind our purchasing Levi's jeans or Fidji perfume or whatever is that we imitate the *desire* of those we see using these products.

Models We Imitate
I make a distinction between heroes and models; heroes are persons who achieve great things and are recognized for their achievements. Models, on the other hands, are people whose looks and behavior (and this includes everything from fashions to use of language to taste in foods and drinks) we imitate— often consciously but sometimes unconsciously. Models may be decidedly unheroic, and may even be evil. Villains are often more attractive and interesting, alas, than decent or ordinary and sometimes even more heroic figures.

If we cannot imitate their actions, we can—and often do—imitate the clothes our models wear, the drinks they consume, the foods they eat, the fashion statements they make (earrings, eyeglass styles, body language, speech mannerisms, and so on). We may start with our parents or teachers and move on to characters from films, television, music videos (God forbid) and other works of popular culture.

Many adolescents, for example, take rock musicians as their role models and thus adopt the "look" of various musicians, some of whom do not lead exemplary lives, it should be said. For a while, a number of years ago, the so-called "grunge" look was popular, due to the popularity of various grunge bands. As new bands with new looks become popular, millions of young men and women, generally in their adolescent years, adopt the look of the members of these bands.

The Power of Images

What an image is actually is rather complicated. We know that the term is connected with the idea of some kind of visual presentation or representation. In semiotic parlance (semiotics being defined earlier as the science of signs), an image can be thought of as a collection of signs. Signs can be understood, as I pointed out earlier in this book, as anything that can be used to stand for something else. One of the founding fathers of semiotics, Saussure, suggested that signs have two components: a sound-image aspect, which he called a signifier, and a concept tied to the sound-image, which he called a signified. The relation between a signifier and a signified is based on convention; that is, it is arbitrary.

When people talk about their "images" they really mean the ideas and associations generated by the way they look, primarily, and act. The way they look would be the signifiers they put together (clothes, hairstyles, body adornments, kinds of glasses, etc.) and the image represents the notions, concepts, ideas or signifieds, semiotically, that people get from their look. What we call "people reading," trying to figure out what people are like when we look at them, is really a matter, from a semiotic perspective, of making sense of or "reading" their signifiers. We read these signifiers so quickly and are so adept at doing so, and do not think, very much, about the process they are involved with. When we look at a photograph, for example, we "read" the photograph in terms of its signs and the same can be said for each moment in a film or television program.

Sometimes, images have an immediate, powerful, visceral impact—based on the nature of the lighting and other aesthetic matters. A number of years ago in a children's program in Japan, there was an image involving a very bright light that traumatized a large number of viewers and had a considerable neurological and psychological impact, for an extended period of time. And the images of 9/11 traumatized the entire United States. So images can have all kinds of effects, from giving us a sense of what a person is like (in one sense of the term) to generating physiological effects of a rather profound nature.

The Power of Information

Information, though we may not think of it as such, often has a controlling (or perhaps, at times, even coercive) power. If we know that X brand of car is more reliable and cheaper to operate than other brands, that bit of information may determine what kind of car we buy. It may not, of course—we may be swayed by our desire for status or by the looks of a car that is not safe and not reliable. If we find out that our lover is cheating on us, that will affect—rather profoundly, one might imagine—our relationship.

In Genesis, it was when Adam and Eve ate from the Tree of Knowledge that their eyes were opened and they recognized that they were naked. When God learned that they had disobeyed him, he threw them out of the Garden of Eden. This story shows the power of information. The story of Adam and Eve, of course, has had an enormous impact upon Western philosophical and religious thought as well as institutions. Let me quote the famous lines:

> The Lord God took the man and placed him in the Garden of Eden, to till it and tend it. And the Lord God commanded the man saying "Of every tree of the garden you are free to eat; but as for the tree of knowledge of good and bad, you must not eat of it; for as soon as you eat of it, you shall die.

Shortly after that, the serpent tempted Eve, who convinced Adam to eat from the tree, as she had done, and that led to

Adam and Eve being expelled from the Garden of Eden and all kinds of dire consequences for men, women and snakes.

We also consider that having certain information and failing to act on the basis of this information can have terrible consequences. Thus, in a celebrated case that took place a number of years ago, a young college student who did nothing when he saw his best friend drag a young girl into a bathroom, where he later raped and killed her, was condemned for not doing anything to save the girl's life. Not doing something when it is expected of you is called "passive aggression," and is a kind of behavior that is destructive of good personal relationships.

The Power of Stories

Most of the texts we are involved with in our daily experiences of popular culture are narratives—stories about individuals and groups that usually involve conflicts and resolutions. Most of the genres we find in our everyday lives and in the mass media are narratives—whether it be conversations, fairy tales, myths, children's stories, fables, commercials, sitcoms, soap operas, detective novels, and so on. Since we are exposed to hundreds of commercials in a given day, we tend to forget or not notice that we are watching narratives. But they have a power over us, in that we see models to imitate and gain insights into the effects of people's behavior.

As Michel de Certeau wrote in *The Practice of Everyday Life* (1984:186)

> From morning to night, narrations constantly haunt streets and buildings. They articulate our existences by teaching us what they must be. They "cover the event," that is to say, they *make* legends (*legenda,* what is to be read and said) out of it. Captured by the radio (the voice is the law) as soon as he awakens, the listener walks all day long through the forest of narrativities from journalism, advertising, and television narrativities that still find time, as he is getting ready for bed, to slip in a few messages under the portals of sleep. Even more than the God told about by the theologians of earlier days, these stories have a providential

and predestining function: they organize in advance our work, our celebrations, and even our dreams. Social life multiplies the gestures and modes of behavior *(im)printed* by narrative models; it...reproduces and accumulates "copies" of stories. Our society has become a recited society, in three senses: it is defined by *stories (recits,* the fables constituted by our advertising and informational media), by *citations* of stories, and by the interminable *recitations* of stories.

Certeau's point is very important: we swim, like fish, in a sea of stories and these stories have the power to shape our ideas and our behavior. These stories are what transmit our culture and give us our culture, or, in technical terms, enculturate us.

As we develop intellectually and emotionally, the kinds of stories we read, hear, are told become increasingly more complex. Thus, we are read children's stories and fairy tales when we are young, and when we are old, we are able to read sophisticated and complex novels. At each stage in our development, there are stories that are available to us and that are appropriate to us. And these stories all do a variety of things—they entertain us, they reflect our beliefs and values, they reinforce some values and neglect others. In short, they teach us, at all times, even though we may not be aware that this is what is happening. Narratives, we may say, are coded messages to us, which help shape our perceptions and influence our thinking and behavior. Let me offer an example of the way in which narratives reflect ideas and stereotypes. I will do this by dealing with a very short form of narratives—jokes.

Jokes as Narratives

Jokes are narratives, we must recall. They can be defined as

> Short, humorous stories,
> meant to create mirthful amusement,
> with punch lines.

In this section, I will deal with a joke about the aged and sexuality. Here, we have humor dealing with matters of considerable importance to people. Humor is a precious gift, one of the few things that we like that is also good for us. The average person laughs more than a dozen times a day (according to figures in the *Harper's Index*) and this laughter serves a number of functions. Happy or mirthful laughter is, strange as it may seem, a mild form of exercise that activates our muscles, increases our heart rate and reduces stress. After we laugh we relax physically for a brief period and this helps diminish tension and anger.

Laughter makes us happy and less self-conscious as we hear jokes about the absurd things people do and speculate about how foolish people (including ourselves) often are. Our jokes, which are the most popular form of humor, often make fun of powerful people and institutions and help liberate us from rigid thinking and obsessive beliefs.

Humor, then, is a force that helps us resist the daily pressures we experience and helps us better accommodate ourselves to the world. The greatest humorists are close to being anarchists; they don't seem to respect anyone or anything and often blast through the boundaries of good taste or conventional thinking. By doing this they help liberate us. But humor also often has an aggressive content to it and in certain situations can be a coercive or directive force. In small groups, humor can push people to think or behave in certain ways--those favored by the person making the jokes and using humor to accomplish certain tasks. A look at the monologues of the great comedians such as Chris Rock and Sarah Silverman shows this combination of aggression and coercion. On fake news shows like *"The Daly Show"* and *"The Colbert Report,"* a number of politicians, performers, celebrities, and groups of one sort or another, are satirized and ridiculed. We see the same thing in cartoons that make fun of various kinds of people and the "insulting" greeting cards that have become very popular. The message is--escape ridicule by conforming to commonly accepted kinds of behavior.

There is still another aspect of humor should be mentioned here, another thing that humor does for us. Humor also often reveals hidden attitudes and unrecognized beliefs that people have, and thus jokes are a useful tool for finding out what's going on in society. A good example of how humor attacks, coerces and reveals hidden notions is found in jokes about sexuality and the aged.

When we look at sex jokes about aged people we tend to find two dominant stereotypes: men who are "too old to cut the mustard anymore" and "sex starved" older women. These stereotypes are codes about the sexual identities of aged men and women. These jokes and others about aged people are an insidious force that oppress their targets by ridiculing them, by insulting them, and by giving them ugly and inaccurate images of themselves. What is disturbing about all this is that humor is conventionally seen as harmless entertainment. Because our humorists are privileged and untouchable, victimized individuals and groups find it difficult to fight back against the stereotypes and images that humorists make popular.

Let me show this by taking a fascinating and complicated joke about sexuality and the aged and showing what it reflects about conventional attitudes on this matter. The joke is "cute" and seemingly harmless, but it spreads a notion about the sexuality of the aged that is quite pernicious. This joke, and jokes like it, reinforces foolish notions many people have about the sexual behavior of men and women in their seventies, eighties and nineties--namely that these people do not and cannot have sex lives. I will call this joke "The Tan."

The Tan

A man goes to Miami Beach for a vacation. After a few days on the beach he looks in the mirror and notices that he has a gorgeous brown tan all over his body except for his penis. He decides to remedy the situation. The next day he gets up early in the morning, walks to a deserted section of the beach, takes off his clothes and lies down. He starts putting sand all over his body until only his penis is exposed to the sun. A short while later a couple of little old ladies walk by. One notices the penis sticking up in the sand. She points it out to her friend. "When I was twenty," she says, "I was scared to death of them. When I was forty, I couldn't get enough of them. When I was sixty, I couldn't get one to come near me...*And now they're growing wild on the beach!*"

I don't tell jokes very well, but when I tell this joke to people, they always find it very amusing. Why might this be?

The most immediate thing we notice about the joke is its sexual content. It is not a "dirty" joke but it is about people's sexuality and that is a subject that people find absorbing, because we are all sexual beings--in addition to whatever else we might be. And we all have a lot of anxiety about our sexuality. The joke deals with the sexual development of the woman telling the joke, as she passes from twenty to forty to sixty, and by implication, the joke deals with the sexuality of women in general. That is, it offers and reinforces conventional notions about women's sexuality, suggesting that they all pass through three stages: fear of sex when young, insatiable desire for sex when middle aged, and inability to find sexual partners when aged.

When the woman was sixty, remember, she "couldn't get one to come near me" because, we are led to assume, aged women are not attractive or desirable. (At what point, we might ask, does a woman become less beautiful and less desirable, and to whom?) This notion about the sexuality of aged women and men is quite absurd, but it is widely held and it is reinforced by jokes like "The Tan." Since it is widely held, it serves to give older men and women a false picture of how they should behave--basically desexualizing them. This image can contribute to aged people giving up on the sexual part of their lives since people tend to act the way they think they are supposed to act.

Ironically, the punch line of the joke represents a kind of paradisiacal state in which penises grow wild on the beach and thus are easily obtainable by everyone in as great a quantity as might be desired. Sexual repression, which Freud postulated as being the price we all pay for civilization, is no longer a significant force, except that the woman who thinks penises are growing wild on the beach is mistaken.

The man in the joke, it could be argued, has unconscious exhibitionist tendencies that are masked by his alleged desire or perhaps even fixation about obtaining an even tan on every part of his body. There may also be an element of narcissism in wanting a "perfect" tan. And this joke also suggests that the woman who recounts her sexual history has regressed to a state in which she either does not know or has forgotten that penises always come connected to a man. They never grow wild at the beach--or any other place.

Jokes actually are more complicated than they seem. In research I've done I've located 45 techniques that can be found in all jokes and other humorous texts. In jokes, it is the punch line, which surprises us, that generates mirthful laughter. If this element of surprise is missing, as in jokes that we've already heard, we no longer find the jokes funny. We make sense of jokes by unconsciously setting up in our minds various relationships. In "The Tan," for example, there is an opposition between the beach (that is, the world of nature) and society, between free sexuality and repression, and between different attitudes towards sex at twenty, forty and sixty, and what we might call "growing wild" sex that is abundant and easily obtainable by all.

The joke involves what might be described as private parts in public places and deals with two characters, each of whom is deficient in some respect. The man who is so driven about his tan is foolish; people don't get tans over every inch of their bodies, or if they wish to do so, they tan themselves in private places where others will not observe their genitals. The woman who sees the man's private parts is mistaken, assuming or hoping, presumably because she is so sex-starved, that she thinks that they are now growing wild on the beach.

Dealing with sexuality and the aged

According to popular stereotypes, "little old ladies" and older men either aren't supposed to be interested in sex or aren't capable of having sex. That is the absurd notion fostered by jokes like "The Tan" and many other jokes about sexuality and the aged. These jokes are populated by sexually undesirable and therefore sex-starved aged women (who haven't yet "renounced" their sexual lives) and aged men who are incapable of performing sexually, of "cutting the mustard."

Our attitudes about sexuality and the aged lead me to suggest that these jokes really deal with unconscious and repressed anxieties young and middle-aged people have about their sexual lives when they grow older. They are probably afraid that they will not be able to enjoy sex then. So they desexualize the aged. By doing this they diminish the sense of loss they fear they will feel.

But when they are aged, unless they've suffered very serious illnesses or been completely brainwashed by ridiculous jokes about sexuality and the aged, they will still be able to find sex pleasurable. Scientific reports show that men and women in their nineties are still capable of having orgasms so we're never too old, it seems, to have sexual lives and to enjoy sex. The joke, then, is on the people who tell jokes ridiculing the idea that aged people can have sex lives.

The Power of Spectacles

One of the ways people become tied more strongly to their social groups, subcultures and cultures is through participation in spectacles such as parades, celebrations, attending football games (or watching them on television), watching international spectacles like the Olympics and participating in similar kinds of activities. The Olympics held in England in 2012 featured over the top beginning and ending spectacles that cost many millions of dollars to put on and attracted huge audiences.
Americans who watched the Olympics broadcast on television cheered for American athletes and were very mindful of the number of Olympic medals won by them.

These spectacles entertain us, but they also reinforce our connection with American culture and society and its values and beliefs. People in large groups have a different sense of themselves and often behave differently than they do when alone.

As the great sociologist Gustave Le Bon explained in his classic work, *The Crowd* (Viking Press, 1960:27) explains:

> The most striking peculiarity presented by a psychological crowd is the following: Whoever be the individuals that compose it, however like or unlike be their mode of life, their occupations, their character, or their intelligence, the fact that they have been transformed into a crowd puts them in possession of a sort of collective mind which makes them feel, think, and act in a manner quite different from that in which each individual of them would feel, think, and act were he in a state of isolation.

At football games, for example, when you are in a stadium with 70,000 or 100,000 fans, you can feel a remarkable sense of excitement and anticipation—and anxiety—as the game progresses.

The Super Bowl

Let me offer some thoughts on one of the most famous sports spectaculars, if not the most important one in the United States, the Super Bowl. I will analyze the Super Bowl from a number of different perspectives. Let me preface these considerations by mentioning that for a couple of years, while stationed in the Army in Washington DC, I wrote high school sports for *The Washington Post.* I was fired from that position for knowing how to spell bizarre (the sports editor didn't) but then taken on week by week until I was released from the Army and went to Europe to do the Grand Tour with money I made from writing sports, I might add. Who knows--maybe my interest in popular culture and the media stems, in part, from that experience--and from a college job I had flipping hamburgers?

Linguistic Analysis

The term "super" in Super Bowl suggests something out of the ordinary, something in the realm of the superlative. Does the existence of things that are "super" somehow diminish the ordinary and give it a second rate status? Are our lives made petty and trivial by the existence of super heroes and super heroines? Or even by so-called "superiors"? (I say so-called because in an individualistic society like we have in America, where authority is not considered valid, the notion of superior beings is not generally accepted. Except for the crazies, that is, who keep waiting for aliens to come from outer space...or who believe they have already here and are walking among us.)

What is unusual about the "Bowl" part of Super Bowl is that the Super Bowl moves around the country, unlike bowls in college sports which are generally located in specific stadiums. Cities are awarded a Super Bowl game and are glad to have them, since they can raise the price of hotel rooms to astronomical levels for the week of the Super Bowl.

Many of the Super Bowls are given to cities like New Orleans and Miami which can handle large crowds and which are tourist attractions on their own right. One of the things that the Super Bowl represents, then, is the synergistic combination of tourism and entertainment--two of the world's mega-industries.   And the Super Bowl is a mass-mediated entertainment that has been around long enough to become part of American folklore.

The two divisions represent different sensibilities. The National division suggests a nation state or a geo-political area. It differs from the American division, which alludes directly to the United States. What are we to make of the fact that teams from the American Football Conference were, for many years, defeated by teams from the National Football Conference? Does this suggest the triumph of a world view, or globalized perspective, focused on nation states, rather than a particularistic Americanist view, is now significant in football as well as commerce? I'll leave that matter for economists and sports theorists to figure out.

A Marxist Perspective
The Super Bowl is the ultimate spectacle in a society of spectacle such as the United States. It is played by alienated millionaires, mostly African-Americans, who move from team to team to obtain even larger payments for their services. The concept of the "team," which suggests some kind of a long-term identification with entities beyond one's self has now almost completely disappeared in American sports--and in most sports played in bourgeois societies. (Unfortunately, the same thing can be said about the concept of community.)

The winning teams from each conference often lose star players from their team and obtain star players from other teams. So professional football teams can now be described as ad hoc assemblages of often alienated and disgruntled millionaires who gather together for a year or so, to try to get to the Super Bowl--to make even more money and to be given a token of their supremacy--a large ring.

The alienation of the players reflects, it can be argued, the alienation of the people who watch the game, the so-called "fans," who identify with teams as a means of escaping from the sense of pettiness and irrelevance in their own non-super lives. The players, who are mostly black, can be looked upon as an exploited racial group, for despite their millions (and not all players make that much money), the owners, who are mostly if not all white, make even more money.

One of the most important functions of the Super Bowl is to deliver the largest audience for any media event to advertisers. The game itself is embedded in a much longer multi-hour spectacle of analysis and discussion, during which time a huge number of television commercials are broadcast. The commercials broadcast during the Super Bowl are, cynics might say, often more entertaining than the game itself.

The Super Bowl is also connected to the real estate market and to the matter of stadium building in cities. Owners of professional football teams threaten cities with abandoning them for other cities that will build stadiums for them.   And they often do abandon cities that are recalcitrant. In addition, a Super Bowl game is often promised to cities that build new stadiums, putting these cities "on the map," as far as the sports world is concerned.

Symbolically, the Super Bowl is similar to all football games in that it deals with taking control of territory, except that the stakes are much higher in the Super Bowl, since the team that takes control of desired territory the most often, and thus scores the most points, wins the championship. Games such as football have often been compared to wars between two armies. But the Super Bowl is pre-eminent because the winner of that game claims to be the world champion football team.

Finally, there is the matter of the Super Bowl as an example of cultural imperialism. The game is broadcast all over the world now, to huge numbers of people who in many cases don't really understand the game and who know almost nothing about the players or the teams. The fact that the Super Bowl game is the largest media event of the year in the United States is yet another testimony to the power of marketing; the whole world has been colonized to see the commercials created by advertising agencies which sell not only products but, indirectly, the self-proclaimed superiority of free enterprise and American bourgeois capitalism.

Super Bowl as Sign System: A Semiotic Perspective.
The fact that Roman Numerals are used to designate which Super Bowl game is being played is an important semiotic sign. Roman Numerals are used to signify importance, status, by connecting an entity to antiquity, to Roman history and ancient civilization. The use of Roman numbers gives football players in the Super Bowl some kind of gladiatorial aura and, in a way, gives the Super Bowl an air of gravity and importance. It is, after all, only a football game.

In the stadium that hosts the Super Bowl, there is the usual brilliance to the colors--the green grass with white stripes every ten yards, the uniforms of the players, the costumes of the cheerleaders, the black and white striped shirts of the officials and their colorful handkerchiefs, the clothes worn by the fans, and so on. And there is signage everywhere--on each player's uniform, in the gestures used by the officials when there are touchdowns, and the advertisements found on the walls of the stadium.

The Super Bowl game--like all football games--is dramatized by the television director who chooses certain shots to focus on some individual or show reactions by players or coaches to a given play. Some plays are shown from three of four different angles and in some cases they are also diagrammed by one of the commentators. I would suggest that the televised version of the Super Bowl, which often employs as many as thirty or so camera crews--many more than ordinary games--is considerably different from the game seen by people at the game.

Television directors can show the same play from several different angles, can zoom in on particular players or coaches and turn the Super Bowl into a psychological thriller. It is this aspect of the televised game, which can approach surrealism, that probably captures the interest of audiences in foreign countries, who generlly know very little about the intricacies of the game itself. The way directors tend to focus on certain players during the game is an unconscious means of strengthening the hyper-individualism that is so dominant in

American culture. The Super Bowl is played by teams but the television broadcast isolates various heroes and fools (those who make mistakes like fumbling the ball) and uses them to create a sense of drama.

The names of football teams are often symbolic and link the teams to historical events or periods, important totems, wild animals and so on. With the rise of self-consciousness in certain groups, such as the Native Americans, the names of teams like the Washington Redskins have now become the subject of considerable controversy. (What happens when the Packers, that is, meat cutters, play the Broncos, that is meat, is anyone's guess but the symbology is not encouraging for the Broncos.)

Psychoanalytic Perspectives on the Super Bowl
The question sports fans asked a number of years ago is whether the Super Bowl involved some ritualistic sacrifice of teams from the American Football League to teams from the National Football League. The NFC was, for many years, a much stronger conference and its teams humiliated AFC teams regularly. Between 1985 and 1997, the AFC has lost 13 Super Bowls in a row. In recent years, the winners and losers, by leagues, have been more balanced. The winners of the Super Bowl since 2004 are listed below:

TEAM	LEAGUE	YEAR
New England Patriots	AFL	2004
New England Patriots	AFL	2005
Pittsburg Steelers	AFL	2006
Indianapolis Colts	AFL	2007
New York Giants	NFL	2008
Pittsburg Steelers	AFL	2009
New Orleans Saints	NFL	2010
Green Bay Packers	NFL	2011
New York Giants	NFL	2012

It is also interesting to consider what is at work in the fans of various teams who so strongly identify with their teams. Some fans have a collector's mentality and need for closure: they pride themselves on never missing a home game for various periods of years. These fans often wear clothes with the logos of their team on it and follow the lives of the team's players and coaches with passionate interest. Because Super Bowls are played in various cities, some fans of conference champions don't get to see their teams in the Super Bowl.

This identification serves to make individuals forget that their lives, as the late Senator Fulbright put it, "are minor events in the ongoing universe." By attaching themselves to their team and to its various heroes, fans give their lives a sense of importance and find an identity. And when their team goes to the Super Bowl, there is a halo effect that is generated.

There is also the matter of the violence that must be considered. This violence is disguised by terms like "tackled" and "sacked" and the rules of the game, which allow for bodily contact. But terms cannot disguise the images of quarterbacks who are shown being sacked, their bodies recoiling in shock with expressions of pain and agony on their faces. Where physical contact ends and violence begins is often difficult to say, but the number of injured players on teams--many of whom can only play because they are given pain killers--is considerable. Because of the number of head injuries in football games, resulting in concussions and brain damage, professional football is facing a crisis that it doesn't know how to resolve yet.

It's interesting to know that more women are battered on Super Bowl Sunday than any other day in America. The violence in the Super Bowl spreads, then, from the game to spectators of the game and their families. Finally, we must consider the boring nature of the game of football. It is a highly routinized and segmented sport, punctuated with huddles, and characterized by relatively short spurts of action, often lasting no more than a few seconds. The game is about controlling territory and about evasion and breaking free of constraints.

When two teams are evenly matched, the question of who will win the game often becomes interesting and heroic actions by this or that player take on a heightened importance. You never can tell what will happen in any football game; some Super Bowl games are very exciting and others are dull. In some games, when a team builds up a huge lead, there is no drama to speak of; there is merely been the matter of the winning team degrading and humiliating the losing team. This forces the commentators to find topics to discuss that are not immediately related to the game.

Sociological Aspects of the Super Bowl
The fact that many of the sites of Super Bowls are tourist and resort areas has already been mentioned; I have suggested that this phenomenon represents the unification of sports (now seen as an entertainment genre) and tourism into a kind of mega-industry. Sports teams and stadiums are now part of the "sell" of cities which wish to attract tourists.

And like tourism, the Super Bowl presents people with an opportunity to display their power and status--first, by having any seat at the Super Bowl, and second, by having a good seat at the Super Bowl. One way people who attend the Super Bowl can measure their status is by calculating how close they were to the fifty yard line...or wherever the "best" seats in the stadium are. The high and mighty, of course, are in boxes where they do not have to mingle with the *hoi polloi*.

Super Bowl Sunday, as it is called, represents the power of media to take a commercial entertainment media event and turn it into a quasi-official national holiday. The Super Bowl is the biggest media sports even of the year in America. Unlike the World Series, the Super Bowl is only one game--so it commands the attention of the American public, which is subjected to weeks of hype on the event.

The Super Bowl can also be seen as a functional alternative to a religious holiday. In fact, one can argue that the Super Bowl is essentially a transmogrified religious event, full of Saints (especially when New Orleans is playing) and Sinners (those who fumble or drop easy passes). The same passion, the same feverish excitement that one finds in religious celebrations is found in the Super Bowl--at least at the beginning of the game. And sometimes, when there are successful "Hail Mary" passes, at the end of a game, when a form of "salvation" has been achieved. (I don't wish to push this analogy too far, but I don't think I'm stretching things to notice the passion in fans and the various similarities between football and religion. I have discussed this matter in some detail in my book *Media Analysis Techniques*.)

This ritual combat in the Super Bowl reflects American culture's values to a considerable degree.   I'm talking about:

1.   an obsession with winning and being "Number One."
2.   an obsession with status and "class."
3.   an obsession with participating in "history."

Thus, there is a concern with identifying with the championship team and obtaining some kind of a "halo" effect, with a game that is the most important one of the year, and with "being there" physically (that gets the most status points) or vicariously, and watching the game.   Some scholars argue that American popular culture and mass media are the only things that help unify an increasingly diverse American society.   If that is the case, certainly the Super Bowl ranks high if not "number one" on the list of acculturating and socializing media events in America.

Conclusions: A Point After
The Super Bowl is, as Mike Real has argued, a mythic media event.   It is an island of a football game that floats in a huge sea of dialogue and chatter from players, coaches, sports journalists, academics, and fans.   And, of course, commercials. I have given--using a number of different disciplines-- what might be described as a Rashomonian interpretation of the Super Bowl, though it might be argued that this kind of analysis should really be saved for RashoMonday Night Football.

How Concepts Are Defined and How they Affect Us
I will conclude this chapter with a discussion of how concepts are defined and how they affect us.   When we watch a football game or a film or a television program or read a spy story or a mystery or participate in popular culture, one way or another, behind the actions of the characters we can usually find some theme or idea or belief that is connected to them or helps explain them.   And sometimes, to help us, a character in a story, will explain his or her behavior for us and spell it out in

terms of ideas, principles, rules, concepts, whatever. (These are all, as I understand things, tied to codes.)

What is remarkable about concepts is that we make sense of them in a rather convoluted way—we define them in terms of their not being their opposites. This point was made by the great Swiss linguist Ferdinand de Saussure, who I quoted earlier: (1966:117):

> Concepts are purely differential and defined not by their positive content but negatively by their relations with the other terms of the system.

And, as he added, the "most precise characteristic" of these concepts "is in being what others are not." What Saussure was arguing is that we make sense of things in terms of their relations with other terms; in other words, nothing has meaning in itself.

We are always, though we may not be aware of what we are doing, making sense of concepts (as well as characters in stories and their actions) by establishing, in our minds, sets of polar oppositions: win, lose; exciting, dull; happy, sad; poor, rich; hero, villain....and on and on it goes. We make these oppositions because of the nature of language, Saussure argues. He is not saying that everything in life should be seen in terms of blacks and whites but that when it comes to concepts, ideas (and I would add characters), we are forced, by language, to see relationships and the most important one is oppositions.

When we watch football games (which, I would argue, can be seen as narratives or narrative-like) or sitcoms or soaps or spy stories, and so on, we are always "reading" what characters say and do in terms of concepts like hero, villain; good girl, temptress; great guy, jerk. Thus language compels us to search for meaning in terms of relationships and oppositions.

The Power of Music
My last topic involves the power of music to generate strong emotions and feelings. In my analysis of the song "It's All in the Game" I dealt with what might be described as codes or

cultural imperatives in the metaphors found in the song's lyrics. But in addition to the lyrics of a song, which by using rhyme, can have a considerable amount of power, there is also the matter of the melody of the song (or of music, in general) and the beat—especially in rock music, Latin music, and so on.

It's difficult to say why music can generate strong emotional responses. In the case of popular song, we must remember that we have the power of narratives at work, also. These songs tell stories about people that mean something to us. At the gym, where I work out, all the songs seem to be about some aspect of "love" or of feelings created by lost love, new love, what you will. So the stories in songs can move us. But there's more to a song than a story; there's also the melody and the beat. In some songs, the lyrics seem rather stupid if you look at them in their printed form; it is only when you hear the song, and see how the lyrics relate to the melody and the beat, that the song makes sense.

As James Lull writes in *Popular Music and Communication: 2nd Edition* (Sage, 1992: 3,4):

> Perhaps to a greater extent than any other art form, popular music has the ability to help shape the consciousness of its audience through sheer thematic repetition. Songs become popular when certain melodic components (riffs or choruses) catch the attention of the public. These recognizable elements of popular songs are also called "hooks," referring to their ability to capture and hold the interest of listeners. The hook is usually repeated several times within a song. "Dance" radio stations and club deejays often superimpose the hook of one song over instrumental fills of other songs, thereby further increasing its impact. And, unlike any other media form, the top "hits" in music are played with great repetition on radio stations, further transmitting the fundamental information contained in the songs to a large audience. Popular music sends particular musical and lyrical fragments deep into the society for the duration of its first run popularity through repetition, then reappears with systematic frequency as "oldies."

We see, then, that because of a variety of factors—repetition, the catchy nature of the hook, the lyrics, the beat--music (and especially popular music) has a uniquely powerful hold on many people. I can recall that many years ago, after a week at my gym, where Paula Cole's "Where Have all the Cowboy's Gone" was played over and over again, I started wondering where they had gone myself. (This song exists, it turns out, in three different edited versions: 3:54, 4:17 and 3:47 minutes.) I should point out that I listen to classical music all the time and it, even though it is generally without lyrics, classical music has a remarkable power to stir my emotions. And, as anyone who has ever attended a rock concert or a classical music concert knows, the emotions of audiences who attend these concerts.

Allan Bloom, a conservative critic of American culture, described the influence of rock music on American youth as follows (Quoted in *the Wall Street Journal,* May 2, 1983):

> The education of children had escaped their parents, no matter how hard they tried to prevent it. The most powerful formative influence on children between 12 and 18 is not the school, not the church, not the home, but rock music and all that goes with it. It is not an elevating but a leveling influence. The children have as their heroes banal, drug and sex ridden guttersnipes who foment rebellion not only against parents but against all noble sentiments. This is the emotional nourishment they ingest in these precious years. It is the real junk food. One thing I have no difficulty teaching students today is the passage in the "Republic" where Socrates explains that control over music is control over character and that the rhythm and the melody are more powerful than the words. They do not especially like Socrates' views on music, but they understand perfectly what he is about and the importance of the issue.

You may not agree with Bloom's assessment of rock music but his point, taken from Socrates, about its power and influence and of the importance of rhythm and melody is hard to argue with—especially since the words in many rock music songs are hard to hear and understand. I would suggest, however, that in many cases, the words to songs are also important and have a powerful effect on listeners.

We also can see the power of music at work in religious services, in which songs play an important role in giving people a sense of community and a sense of the divine. In some cases, people sing songs in Latin or Hebrew and don't necessarily know the meaning of the words they are singing. But the melodies are so beautiful (many of the Hebrew songs happen to be in a minor key, and minor keys seem to have a remarkable power to stir the emotions) that people derive a great sense of pleasure and satisfaction from singing these songs.

Conclusions

In this chapter I have tried to suggest that popular culture and the mass media that carries various forms or kinds of popular culture are not simple entertainments that wash off our minds and consciousness the way water washes off a duck's back. We are, more than we may imagine, profoundly affected by popular culture, which has now, in many cases, become a more dominant socializing influence on us than our parents. We are affected by learning codes that are found in these texts and which have the power to shape our thinking.

What we must do is learn how to interpret popular culture and learn how to understand it's power, so we can cope with it, so we can make rational and intelligent decisions about life and our behavior.   There are, I am suggesting, all kinds of unconscious imperatives and effects from popular culture that we must learn how to recognize and deal with. If we don't, we may go through life believing that "love is a game" and all kinds of other ridiculous and frequently self-destructive things.

The 95-5 Split

Consciousness is crucial in daily life for many obvious reasons. However, an important fact and one of the key principles of this book is the 95-5 split. At least 95 percent of all cognition occurs below awareness in the shadows of the mind while, at most, only 5 percent occurs in high-order consciousness. Many disciplines have confirmed this insight. John Haugeland explains this idea eloquently:

> *Thus, compared to "unconscious processing"...conscious thinking is conspicuously laborious and slow—not a lot faster than talking, in fact. What's more, it is about as difficult to entertain consciously two distinct trains of thought at the same time as it is to engage in two distinct conversations at once; consciousness is in some sense a linear or serial process in contrast to the many simultaneously cognitions that are manifest in [unconscious action].*

To quote Edelman and Tononi..."Unconscious aspects of mental activity, such as motor and cognitive routines, and so-called unconscious memories, intentions, and expectations play a fundamental role in shaping and directing our conscious experience." (Pages 50-51)

> Gerald Zaltman, *How Customers Think: Essential Insights Into The Mind of the Market*

Coda

In this book I have raised the subject of the role of culture codes in our everyday lives and in our societies. Just as Freud posited an unconscious in individuals that, below their level of awareness, shapes much of their behavior, I suggest that there are these culture codes that generally are unconscious but which shape many of our thoughts and various aspects of our behavior. We can understand Freud's notions by suggesting that the psyche is like an iceberg. At the top, floating above the water, is the part of iceberg we see. If you look down around six feet or so you can dimly make out a section of the iceberg that corresponds to what Freud called our pre-conscious. But around ninety percent of the iceberg exists below the pre-conscious and cannot be seen. This is the unconscious and it plays a major role in our lives.

Research by some neuroscientists suggest there is what they call the "active unconscious" that shapes much of our decision making, even if we are not aware that this is the case. Our unconscious often does a better job of helping us make some decisions than our conscious minds. The quote from Gerald Zaltman, at the beginning of this chapter, suggests that 95 percent of all cognition occurs below awareness.

One way of thinking about these culture codes is that many of them become habits. Habits are useful because they save us from the need to make decisions all the time about the things we commonly do. If you develop a habit about how to answer a phone call, you don't have to think, at each call, "what shall I say?" So habits are examples of culture codes that are based on conscious decisions, usually. But, as I've explained, most of the codes that shape our thinking, feeling and behavior are unconsciously absorbed and "imprinted upon us" as we grow up. If you grow up in the United States, chances are you say "Hello" when you answer the phone. In Italy, you would say "Pronto" which means "ready."

I've always been fascinated by the many differences between countries, and used the quotes from Pico Iyer about Saigon and Reykjavik to show how different cultures can be. Research I conducted in the Sixties showed that there were considerable differences in terms of attitudes towards authority in Italian and American comic strips that were similar in terms of the kinds of characters they had and when they were published. Italian comics accepted authority as valid while American comics rejected authority, and these comic strips reflected values and beliefs that were typical of each country at the time I conducted my research.

Bibliography

This bibliography contains many sources that will of interest to you in doing research on culture codes, culture, popular culture, the media, and related concerns.

Abrams, M. H. (1958). *The Mirror and the Lamp: Romantic Theory and the Critical Condition.* New York: W.W. Norton..

Adatto, K. (1993). *Picture perfect: The art and artifice of public image making.* New   York: Basic Books.

Bakhtin, M. M. (1981). *The dialogic imagination: Four essays* (M. Holquist, Ed.; C. Emerson & M. Holquist, Trans.). Austin: University of Texas Press.

Barthes, R. (1972). *Mythologies.* New York: Hill & Wang.

Berger, A. A. (1976b). *The TV-guided American.* New York: Walker.

Berger, A. A. (1989). *Seeing is believing: An introduction to visual communication.* Mountain View, CA: Mayfield.

Berger, A. A. (1990). *Agitpop: Political culture and communication theory.* New Brunswick, NJ: Transaction.

Berger, A. A. (1992). *Popular culture genres: Theories and texts.* Newbury Park, CA: Sage.

Berger, A. A. (1997). *Narratives in popular culture, media, and everyday life.* Thousand Oaks, CA: Sage.

Berger, A. A. (2002). *Video games: A popular culture phenomenon.* New Brunswick, NJ: Transaction.

Berger, A. A. (2005). *Making Sense of Media: Key Texts in Media and Cultural Studies.* Malden, MA: Blackwell.

Berger, A. A. (2006). *50 Ways to Understand Communication.* Lanham, MD: Rowman & Littlefield.

Berger, A. A. (2012). *Media and society: A critical perspective.* 3rd edition. Lanham, MD: Rowman & Littlefield.

Berger, A. A. (2012). *Media Analysis Techniques.* 4th edition. Thousand Oaks, CA: Sage.

Bernstein, B. (1977). *Class, codes and control.* London: Routledge & Kegan Paul.

Bettelheim, B. (1977). *The uses of enchantment: The meaning and importance of fairy tales.* New York: Vintage.

Bolter, J. D., & Grusin, R. (2000). *Remediation: Understanding new media.* Cambridge: MIT Press.

Bourdieu, P. "Intellectual Field and Creative Project," *Social Science Information*. April, 1969. Pp 89-119.

Brenner, C. (1974). *An elementary textbook of psychoanalysis*. Garden City, NY: Doubleday.

Brooker, P. (1999). *Cultural theory: A glossary*. London: Arnold.

Caudwell, C. (1971). *Studies and further studies in a dying culture*. New York: Monthly Review Press.

Certeau, Michel de. (1984). *The Practice of Everyday Life*. (Transl. by Steven Rendall). Berkeley, CA: University of California Press.

Culler, J. (1976). *Structuralist poetics: Structuralism, linguistics and the study of literature*. Ithaca, NY: Cornell University Press.

Csikszentmihalyi, M. (1990). *Flow: The psychology of optimal experience*. New York: Harper & Row.

Danesi, M. (2002). *Understanding media semiotics*. London: Arnold.

Dichter, E. (1960). *The strategy of desire*. London: Boardman.

Dichter, E. (1964). *Handbook of consumer motivations: The psychology of the world of objects*. New York: McGraw-Hill.

Dorfman, A. and Mattelart, A. (1984) *How To Read Donald Duck*. Amsterdam: International General.

Doyle, A.C. (1982). *A Study in Scarlet*. New York: Penguin.

Dressler, D. (1969). *Sociology: The study of human interaction*. New York: Knopf.

Durham, M. G. and Kellner, D.M. (Eds.). *Media and Cultural Studies: KeyWorks*. Malden, MA: Blackwell.

Durkheim, É. (1965). *The elementary forms of religious life* (J. W. Swain, Trans.). New York: Free Press. (Original work published 1915)

Eco, U. (1972, Autumn). Towards a semiotic inquiry into the television message. *Working Papers in Cultural Studies, 3*.

Eco, U. (1976). *A theory of semiotics*. Bloomington: Indiana University Press.

Eidelberg, L. (1968). *The encyclopedia of psychoanalysis*. New York: Macmillan.

Eliade, M. (1961). *The sacred and the profane: The nature of religion* (W. R. Trask, Trans.). New York: Harper & Row. (Original work published 1957)

Engels, F. (1972). Socialism: Utopian and scientific. In R. C. Tucker (Ed.), *The Marx-Engels reader*. New York: W. W. Norton.

Enzenberger, H. M. (1974). *The consciousness industry: On literature, politics and the media*. New York: Seabury.

Erikson, E. (1968). *Identity, youth, and crisis*. New York: W. W. Norton.

Fairchild, H.P. (Ed.) (1967). *Dictionary of Sociology and Related Sciences*. Totawa, NJ: Littlefield, Adams.

Freud, S. (1962). *Civilization and its discontents*. New York: W. W. Norton.

Freud, S. (1963). *Character and culture* (P. Rieff, Ed.). New York: Collier.

Freud, S. (1965). *The interpretation of dreams* (J. Strachey, Trans.). New York: Avon. (Original work published 1900)

Friedson, E. (1953). Communication research and the concept of the mass. *American Sociological Review, 18*(3).

Frith, S. (1981). *Sound effects: Youth, leisure, and the politics of rock 'n' roll*. New York: Pantheon.

Fromm, E. (1957). *The forgotten language: An introduction to the understanding of dreams, fairy tales and myths.* New York: Grove.

Fromm, E. (1962). *Beyond the chains of illusion: My encounter with Marx and Freud.* New York: Simon & Schuster.

Girard, R. (1991). *A Theater of Envy: William Shakespeare .* New York: Oxford University Press.

Gitlin, T. (1989, July-August). Postmodernism defined, at last! *Utne Reader,* pp. 52–58, 61.

Glasgow University Media Group. (1980). *More bad news.* London: Routledge & Kegan Paul.

Grotjahn, M. (1966). *Beyond laughter: Humor and the subconscious.* New York: McGraw-Hill.

Hall, S. (1997). Introduction. In S. Hall (Ed.), *Representation: Cultural representations and signifying practices.* London: Sage.

Haug, W. F. (1986). *Critique of commodity aesthetics: Appearance, sexuality, and advertising in capitalist society.* Minneapolis: University of Minnesota Press.

Haug, W. F. (1987). *Commodity aesthetics, ideology, and culture.* New York: International General.

Henderson, J. L. (1964). Ancient myths and modern man. In C. G. Jung with M.-L. von Franz, J. L. Henderson, J. Jacobi, & A. Jaffé, *Man and his symbols* (pp.-104–157). Garden City, NY: Doubleday.

Hinsie, L. E., & Campbell, R. J. (1970). *Psychiatric dictionary.* New York: Oxford University Press.

hooks, b. (1992). *Black looks: Race and representation.* Boston: South End.

Horton, P., & Hunt, C. (1972). *Sociology.* New York: McGraw-Hill.

Iyer, P. (1993). *Falling Off the Map: Some Lonely Places of the World.* New York: Vintage.

Jakobson, R. (1988). Linguistics and poetics. In D. Lodge (Ed.), *Modern criticism and theory: A reader* (pp.-32–57). New York: Longman.

Jameson, F. (1991). *Postmodernism; or, The cultural logic of late capitalism.* Durham, NC: Duke University Press.

Jones, E. (1949). *Hamlet and Oedipus.* New York: W. W. Norton.

Jung, C. G. (1964). Approaching the unconscious. In C. G. Jung with M.-L. von Franz, J. L. Henderson, J. Jacobi, & A. Jaffé, *Man and his symbols* (pp.-18–103). Garden City, NY: Doubleday.

Katz, E., Blumler, J. G., & Gurevitch, M. (1979). Utilization of mass communication by the individual. In G. Gumpert & R. Cathcart (Eds.), *Inter/media* New York: Oxford University Press.

Kubey, R. W. (1996). Television dependence, diagnosis, and prevention: With commentary on video games, pornography, and media education. In T. M. MacBeth (Ed.), *Tuning in to young viewers: Social science perspectives on television* (pp.-221–259). Thousand Oaks, CA: Sage.

Lacan, J. (1966). *Écrits: A selection* (A. Sheridan, Trans.). New York: W. W. Norton.

Lakoff, G., & Johnson, M. (1980). *Metaphors we live by.* Chicago: University of Chicago Press.

Lazere, D. (1977). Mass culture, political consciousness, and English studies. *College English, 38,* 751–767.

LeBon, Gustav. (1885/1960). *The Crowd: A Study of the Popular Mind.* New York: Viking Press.

Lefebvre, H. (1984). *Everyday life in the modern world.* New Brunswick, NJ: Transaction. (Original work published 1968)

Lesser, S. O. (1957). *Fiction and the unconscious.* Boston: Beacon.

Lessig, L. (2001). *The future of ideas: The fate of the commons in a connected world.* New   York: Random House.

Lifton, Robert. (1974). *Who is More Dry? Heroes of Japanese Youth.* In Berger, A. A. (Ed.) *About Man.* Dayton, OH: Pflaum.

Lévi-Strauss, C. (1967*). Structural anthropology.* Garden City, NY: Doubleday.

Lotman, J. M. (1977). *The structure of the artistic text* (G. Lenhoff & R. Vroon, Trans.). Ann Arbor: Michigan Slavic Contributions.

Lowenthal, L. (1944). Biographies in popular magazines. In P. F. Lazarsfeld   & F. Stanton (Eds.), *Radio research 1943–43.* New York: Duell, Sloan & Pearce.

Lull, J. (1991). *Popular Music and Communication.* Thousand Oaks, CA: Sage.

Lyotard, J.-F. (1984). *The postmodern condition: A report on knowledge* (G. Bennington & B. Massumi, Trans.). Minneapolis: University of Minnesota Press.

Mandell, A. J. (1974, October). A psychiatric study of professional football. *Saturday Review/World*

Mannheim, K. (1936). *Ideology and Utopia: An Introduction to the Sociology of Knowledge.* New York: Harcourt Brace..

Marx, K. (1964). *Selected writings in sociology and social philosophy* (T. B. Bottomore & M. Rubel, Eds.; T. B. Bottomore, Trans.). New York: McGraw-Hill.

McChesney, R. W. (1999). *Rich media, poor democracy: Communication politics in dubious times.* Urbana: University of Illinois Press.

McLuhan, M. (1964). *The mechanical bride: Folklore of industrial man.* Boston: Beacon.

McQuail, D., & Windahl, S. (1993). *Communication models for the study of mass communication* (2nd ed.). New York: Longman.

Messaris, P. (1994). *Visual literacy: Image, mind, and reality.* Boulder, CO: Westview.

Monaco, J. (1977). *How to read a film.* New York: Oxford University Press.

Murray, J. (1997). *Hamlet on the holodeck: The future of narrative in cyberspace.* Cambridge: MIT Press.

Pines, M. (1982, October 13). How they know what you really mean. *San Francisco Chronicle.*

Propp, V. (1968). *Morphology of the folktale.* Austin: University of Texas Press. (Original work published 1928)

Provenzo, E. (1997). Video games and the emergence of interactive media. In S. R. Steinberg & J. L. Kincheloe (Eds.), *Kinder-culture: The corporate construction of childhood.* Boulder, CO: Westview.

Radway, J. A. (1991). *Reading the romance: Women, patriarchy, and popular literature.* Chapel Hill: University of North Carolina Press.

Rapaille, Clothaire. (2006). *The Culture Code.* New York: Broadway Books.

Real, M. R. (1977). *Mass-mediated culture.* Englewood Cliffs, NJ: Prentice Hall.

Saussure, F. de. (1966). *A course in general linguistics* (W. Baskin, Trans.). New   York: McGraw-Hill. (Original work published 1915)

Signorielli, N., & Gerbner, G. (1988). Introduction. In N. Signorielli & G. Gerbner (Comps.), *Violence and terror in the mass media: An annotated bibliography.* Westport, CT: Greenwood.

Thompson, M., Ellis, R., & Wildavsky, A. (1990). *Cultural theory.* Boulder, CO: Westview.

von Franz, M.-L. (1964). The process of individuation. In C. G. Jung with M.-L. von Franz, J. L. Henderson, J. Jacobi, & A. Jaffé, *Man and his symbols* (pp.-158–229). Garden City, NY: Doubleday.

Warner, W. L. (1953). *American life: Dream and reality.* Chicago: University of Chicago Press.

White, L.   (1973). *The Concept of Culture.*   Minneapolis, MN: Burgess Publishing

Wildavsky, A. (1989). *Choosing preferences by constructing institutions: A cultural theory of preference formation.* Presidential address delivered at the annual meeting of the American Political Science Association.

Williams, R. (1977). *Marxism and literature.* Oxford: Oxford University Press.

Zeman, J. J. (1977). Peirce's theory of signs. In T. A. Sebeok (Ed.), *A perfusion of signs.* Bloomington: Indiana University Press.

 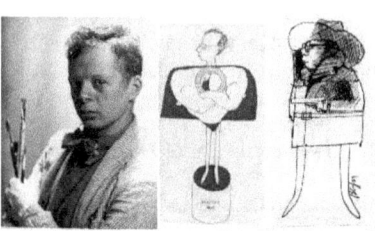 

Lino block   Artists as young man   Decoder Man   Secret Agent   Playboy

Arthur Asa Berger is professor emeritus of Broadcast and Electronic Communication Arts at San Francisco State University, where he taught between 1965 and 2003. He graduated in 1954 from the University of Massachusetts in Amherst, Massachusetts, where he majored in literature and minored in philosophy and art. He received a Master's Degree in journalism (but also studied at the Writers Workshop) from the University of Iowa in 1956. He was elected to the University of Iowa School of Journalism and Mass Communication's "Hall of Fame" in 2009. He received a Ph.D. in American Studies from the University of Minnesota in 1965. He wrote his dissertation on the comic strip *Li'l Abner.*

In 1963 he had a Fulbright to Italy and lectured at the University of Milan. In 1983-84 he was visiting professor at the Annenberg School for Communication at the University of Southern California. He has also taught at Heinrich Heine University in Dusseldorf, Germany, the Hong Kong Polytechnic University in Hong Kong, Jinan University in Guangzhou and Tsinghua University in Beijing, China. Over the years has lectured in thirty countries such as England, Denmark, Norway, Sweden, Peru, France, Germany, Finland, Italy, Turkey, Tunisia, Morocco, Russia and Ukraine. He lectured on media and semiotics in Argentina in August/September 2012 as a Fulbright Senior Specialist.

He has published more than one hundred articles in publications such as *The Journal of Communication, Society, Rolling Stone, Semiotica,* the *San Francisco Chronicle* and the *Los Angeles Times* and more than sixty books on media, popular culture, humor, and tourism. Among his books are: *Li'l Abner: A Study in American Satire; Pop Culture; Understanding American Icons; Signs in Contemporary Culture: An Introduction to Semiotics; The Golden Triangle: an Ethno-Semiotic Tour of Present-Day India; What Objects Mean; Media and Society; Media and Communication Research Methods; Making Sense of Media; Bloom's Morning; Ads, Fads and Consumer Culture;* and *Shop 'Til You Drop.* His work on media has focused on the impact of media and popular culture on individuals and on American consumer culture. He has also written a number of academic murder mysteries such as *Postmortem for a Postmodernist, The Mass Comm Murders: Five Media Theorists Self-Destruct,* and *Durkheim is Dead: Sherlock Holmes is Introduced to Sociological Theory.* His books have been translated into eight languages and fourteen of his books have been translated into Chinese.

Dr. Berger is married and has two children and four grandchildren. He lives in Mill Valley, California and enjoys foreign travel, lecturing on American culture, and dining in ethnic restaurants. He can be reached at: arthurasaberger@gmail.com. Latest article on my career as writer/artists/secret agent: http://www.enculturation.net/writing-myself-into-existence lete this text prior to use.

www.ingramcontent.com/pod-product-compliance
Lightning Source LLC
Chambersburg PA
CBHW072320290526
45794CB00002B/717